EMBRACING

EMBRACING

Life

ONE STAGE AT A TIME

ADELA DALTO MORAUX

For permissions, licensing, or special discounts on bulk orders, please contact: info@mlmundo.com

ISBN (print): 979-8-9994462-0-6
ISBN (ebook): 979-8-9994462-1-3

Book design and production by www.AuthorSuccess.com

Library of Congress Control Number: 2025920019

Printed in the United States of America

ML Mundo Publishing
8 Atkinson Dr. #575
Doylestown, PA. 18901
info@mlmundo.com

For

Sylvia, Dina, and Michelle

Contents

Introduction

I have always felt that I've lived an adventurous life, from my first trip to Mexico at nine years old to my latest trip to sing in Cuba weeks away from my seventieth birthday. I've traveled to over forty-two countries so far, and my travels show no signs of stopping. When I wasn't singing in a wonderful city somewhere in the world, I was home in my Columbus Avenue apartment on the Upper West Side of Manhattan, working on a project, writing lyrics, or learning new melodies.

If I needed motivation, all I had to do was take the elevator down and step out into the urban sights, sounds, and aromas—both good and bad. There are plenty of fancy clothing shops, restaurants, and nightclubs, adding plenty of adventure to any stroll. With museums filled with a wide range of treasures, schools for curious minds, and people from diverse cultures strolling along the avenue, the city buzzes with life, rich history, and endless inspiration. This had been my neighborhood from 1979 to 2015.

Just outside the front door of my building, I had Central Park to the left, and to the right, I had Riverside Park that ran along the mighty Hudson River. A few buildings down was the Claremont Riding Academy. I can still remember Sunday mornings, when traffic was quiet— the sound of the clip-clop, clip-clop of metal horseshoes striking the pavement as a horse ambled past below my eighth-floor window, carrying its rider into the trails in Central Park. I found it to be such a calming, rhythmic sound—until it would get drowned out by booming bass vibrations blasting beats from an open car trunk. We also had helicopter tours that would swoop low over the rooftops of our buildings, rattling the windows, along with everything else in my apartment. My eardrums would flutter from the vibrations coming from the rotors until finally the city put a stop to loud disturbances. No longer would you hear music blaring out of the many bars, either. By 2007, the city that never sleeps was now closing early and sending people home.

My senses absorbed a wide range of information from living in New York City, enriched by my exciting and educational travels around the world, which fueled my inspiration. Back at my desk, I would continue to focus on my projects, including some that I hadn't completed, as my brain is always creating something new. I'd start by laying down my thoughts in bullet points, then push the notebook to the back burner, saving it for when I could get back to it because a phone call would come in with a singing gig somewhere in the world. Whatever I was working on would have to stop until I was free again, while the gig took center stage. I was always ready to take the stage and eager to explore a new city or a new country.

I never dreamed about being a professional singer; I just happened to be at the right place at the right time. Additionally, being married to a musician was also beneficial. I never thought about all that it takes to be on stage. When we moved to New York City in 1974, I was one of a couple of young Latina singers being called for the Spanish commercials. Soon after, I stepped on stage to cover a weekly gig in a nightclub for a friend who was pregnant. That's how I started, and there was plenty to learn along the way.

Whether you can make it as a professional singer depends on the type of voice you have and the repertoire you choose to develop your breathing techniques. You need to vocalize every day and practice reading music to learn a new song in case you are called to perform someone else's music for a recording or performance. For your own gigs, you need to have proper song selection for the audience you will face, musical arrangements for the musicians, memorize the lyrics, and plan the outfits you will need. You can't forget the jewelry, shoes (comfortable, sexy shoes), and, of course, the hair and nails.

Then there's the business side of the music, which is so complicated today—learning how to collect your earnings from the publishing of your original music, whether through recordings and social media, can be overwhelming. It's also essential to have a manager and a publishing company, which is key to growing your audience and planning out your goals. It's not easy to find someone willing to dedicate the time and money it takes to help develop your career. Using social platforms has worked well for several independent artists, but managing them takes a lot of time—time you need to practice your craft.

However, when you're passionate about being a musical artist, you're mainly grateful to be performing. Unless you've taken a business course, you don't think about the financial gain early in your career. Nonetheless, situations can come up that can make you think twice about your dream, especially when you've been performing for a while and you still don't see any savings in your bank account.

I recall being called to stand in for Cuban singer and my mentor, Graciela Grillo, because the venue didn't want to pay the $10,000 she demanded. Instead, the venue offered me $350 for two shows, plus two rehearsals. I laughed and told them, "That doesn't even cover my hair and nails."

We negotiated, but after that experience, I decided I needed a second career to help me build my Social Security account and some savings. I was already in my forties, and I certainly didn't want to be known as the mature singer with bad teeth. I wanted health insurance and a dental plan.

Having raised two children as a single mom, I sometimes needed office jobs to cover insurance and supplement my income between traveling gigs, singing in local jazz clubs, or recording commercials. I even taught singing lessons.

In the 1970s, 1980s, and early 1990s, singing on commercials was a highly profitable endeavor. The contracts had to be approved by the Local 802 musicians' union, and the checks would arrive in the mail. That was the best payday—finding a stack of checks in my mailbox. There was a special joy in turning the key and finding envelopes from the union. There was a time when singers and musicians could earn an excellent living, but these opportunities gradually decreased as some commercials no longer went through the union. Additionally, producers began utilizing the latest computer programs to create music that could replicate any instrument, and they could also employ autotune to correct pitch issues if their non-professional singers (sometimes family or girlfriends) were not quite in tune.

When my two sons went off to college, I still had to support them financially until they graduated and started their careers, so it was a financial struggle most of the time. Performing can be a glamorous career. Wearing flashy clothing, receiving applause that becomes addictive, and meeting a lot of people in front and behind the stage make it all so exciting . . . but at what cost?

After the venue experience, which was very successful, with the audience applauding me and the producers having me close the show on the second night following my exciting and powerful performance, I realized that I would only have limited success without a strong manager and a record company behind me. Traveling outside the country pays well, but you need to supplement your income, and it isn't easy to hold another job that allows you to travel. When we experienced the 9/11 terrorist attack on the Twin Towers, several of my performances were canceled as the world waited to see what would happen next.

After the attack, I developed a fear of traveling alone, as I had to do on many occasions when promoters would offer me jobs to sing outside of the United States. While working on a cruise ship, I was stalked by an employee who would step out from behind the hidden doors of the employee service halls. On another occasion, while driving in New Jersey after a gig, I got so lost driving (there was no GPS back then) that I had to ask someone walking on the street for directions at 3:00 in the morning. In exchange, I had to agree to give the person a ride and he asked for some money before he got out of my car.

I took many chances, even walking home a few blocks after parking my car in my neighborhood, when it was hazardous in the '70s and '80s in NYC. It was now a new decade, 2000, and time to reevaluate my profession. I was now a widow, having raised my two sons in New York City, and they were now out in the world creating their own space.

My curiosity was calling, seeking more information beyond the music world. It was time to enter a new stage in my life. I was open to learning and accepting new challenges that would enrich my adventures, whether it was traveling, pursuing a degree, or taking the time to investigate when my creative juices flowed from my soul. It was time to explore a new path and see what adventures awaited me, including heartache, and even a second marriage at sixty.

My stage continues to lighten up. But whether I'm in front of a microphone or behind a desk, traveling or sharing a story, I've learned that the real performance is how we show up for ourselves—day by day, moment to moment, and ready to take on the challenge of the day.

CHAPTER 1

My First Adventure Was Terrifying

Here we were, on this narrow, rocky, treacherous path high on a mountain pass. It could have been Espinazo del Diablo, the Devil's Backbone, one of the many mountains of the Sierra Madre in Mexico. It was 8,000 feet above sea level and had many narrow, winding roads. The two-lane paved cement road was poorly maintained, with loose stones here and there that had fallen off the face of the mountain. The road didn't have a single guardrail, and it didn't appear to be on anyone's maintenance schedule. No way! Some sections of the road looked like it was built for donkeys, not for the modern cars that were now being assembled in the American car factories of Mexico in the early 1960s.

Traveling slowly along sections of the rocky, winding road, my heart pounded at the thought that we might go over the edge at the next curve. A couple of times, my dad had to stop the car to get out and move some rocks that were too large to drive over, or risk ripping the muffler off. I looked out of my window and couldn't see the ground below. I shrieked. My sister said, "Stop looking out and lean in."

I rested my head on my mother's shoulder, and I kept my eyes tightly shut while I prayed to my guardian angel to be ready to catch me if we lost control and went over the edge.

I thought, *I'm only nine years old. I'm too young to die.* I prayed to my angel to catch me if we came tumbling down, catching all the jagged rocks of the mountain with our brand-new station wagon as it plunged down toward the tiny houses in the village below. Between my prayers and my thoughts, I would peek up from my window at the wide-open blue sky, only to see some black vultures flying just above us, as if they were waiting for some fresh flesh to hit the ground.

We were heading to the city of Villahermosa in the state of Tabasco, from our home in East Chicago, Indiana, to start a new life on our small ranch in Southern Mexico.

The drive began by crossing the state line into Illinois, and after about six hours, we were cruising alongside the great 630-foot-tall Gateway Arch in Saint Louis, Missouri, which was known as the gateway to the West. It was the confirmation that we were headed in the right direction, as I had remembered the mighty steel arch on other vacations. We would drive past it each summer, heading down to Texas to visit my maternal grandparents, where sometimes my parents would leave us behind while they traveled across the border to shop for the day. Other times, they would travel further to Villahermosa so my father could visit with family. But now, on this trip, we were heading all the way south—together.

I was excited that we were now on our way to Mexico. I helped pack my favorite dress, my favorite bag of candy, and other carefully selected clothes into my duffel bag, which fit under the seat in the car. I had daydreamed about what it must be like to attend school, go to the movies, or make friends, since I didn't speak the language well. Now, finally, all of us were sitting in the crowded car. My mother sat in the back seat with my youngest brother,

Louie, on her lap, between my oldest sister, Sylvia, and me. Our baby sister sat on Sylvia's lap. We used to joke that Sylvia was her mother because she wouldn't sit with anyone else, or she'd cry.

There were no bucket seats back then, so Jesse, who was five, sat in front between my father, the driver, and my eldest brother, Joe. Fortunately, we had a new 1961 red Rambler Cross Country station wagon, which had just enough space to fit us all. There was even space in the back section where the young ones could sleep or sit to play with their toy horses around the luggage that was strategically placed. We would take turns sitting between Joe and Dad in the front seat.

I looked forward to my turn so I could manage the radio, trying to find some pop music to keep us distracted from the growing heat as we traveled further south. I searched for music my sister and I could sing along with, like Chubby Checker's "Let's Twist," or Paul Anka's "Put Your Head on My Shoulder," The Drifters' "There Goes My Baby," and of course, there was "Donna" by Ritchie Valens. My sister and I were in love with Ritchie Valens's voice. He had the darkest pompadour hairstyle, complete with the curl. We sang a cappella since I could only find local Mexican music, until my father said, "Ya, enough."

My father had made the trip south many times, even before I was born. He had been part of the Bracero Program—a guest worker agreement between the U.S. and Mexico designed to address labor shortages after World War II, especially in agriculture. Braceros also helped build the Southern Pacific Railroad before many moved on to other jobs. The term *bracero* comes from *brazo*, meaning "arm," symbolizing manual labor. The program ended in 1964. He often shared stories about his experiences working across the United States.

My father had rich, dark, wavy hair, a neatly trimmed mustache, gray-green eyes, and a short but strong build. After all, he was a part-time barber and eventually worked in a steel mill. His appearance stood out—and if he was in the wrong place at the wrong time, he sometimes had to stomach racist comments and threats during his travels. He always knew where to stop for food, gas, and bathrooms—usually just before entering a town where he'd had an unfriendly experience.

After about twenty-five hours—stopping only for a few short naps, bathroom breaks, and eating by the roadside—we finally arrived in Elsa, Texas, a dry, dusty town an hour from the Rio Grande River, which divides the US and Mexico. It was my mother's hometown. I could recognize that we were just a few blocks away when we passed the cotton gin, with its tall silo and bits of cotton caught on the fencing surrounding the property. The area was once filled with cotton fields, where we would sometimes work during our summer vacations to earn extra money for school supplies and shoes. The steel mill strike of 1959, which lasted from July through November, didn't cause us much hardship because my parents worked in the fields during the strike. The fields were always a lifesaver until the job at the mill increased salaries, and with my father's side hustle of cutting hair, it eliminated the need to work in the fields.

Still, my mother, who had worked in the fields as a child for many years, would sometimes feel nostalgic and want to join her friends to pick tomatoes in Indiana, then jar them up for the winter months. We'd get picked up by a neighbor very early in the morning, and we'd all go to work. The men worked at the steel mill and only went to the fields if there was a strike at the plant. To this day, when my husband brings home tomatoes on the vine, the aroma draws me back to the memory of the rich earth and the sharp, fresh scent of the plants, inviting me to bite into the juicy flesh of a bright red tomato right there in the field.

As the car finally rolled around the corner, we pulled up in front of the wooden porch, where my grandpa got up from his rusting metal rocking chair to greet us. We stumbled out of the car, stretching our cramped legs, hurrying to hug him, then we ran inside to the kitchen. We followed the aroma of frijoles rancheros and freshly made warm flour tortillas, which always complemented the spicy beans. We visited with our grandparents, and we ate while sitting on the wooden porch floor. Our grandfather, in his rocking chair, loved to share stories of his adventures. I always asked him to tell us about when the Mexican soldiers were in his town, burning houses and killing people to get them off their land, and how he had to hide in the mountains until it was safe to leave. I used to pay close attention to hear if he had embellished the story, because each time I had heard it, it was as if I was hearing it for the first time.

Nightfall came quickly. We spent the night there and continued our journey into Mexico the following morning.

Passing through Mexican customs wasn't easy. Dad had to pay the "mordida"—the bribe—just so the agents would let us cross the border without having to unload everything for inspection to see if we were carrying anything we weren't supposed to bring into the country . . . whatever that was. My dad knew the hustle. He paid the officer, and we continued our journey toward the mountains, heading south.

The drive was hot, but it got even hotter as we tried to sleep for the night in a motel without air conditioning. We couldn't drive at night because there were no lights and the roads were unpredictable.

The next morning, we headed for the final leg of the trip. All was fine until we started traveling up a very intimidating mountain. Reaching the midpoint before heading down on the other side wasn't pleasant. It was not like today, with modern roads and bridges that cut driving time (although it is still perilous).

The road was treacherous, with fallen stones from the face of the mountain. Occasionally, a car would sluggishly drive by. There were sections of the road that were riddled with cracks and potholes, making the ride so hazardous that we were traveling inch by inch. Of course, there were no car seats for my younger siblings. Cars didn't even have seatbelts back then. Imagine if we had gone over a cliff—we wouldn't have been falling gracefully like the brown hawks I saw soaring in the sky, riding the currents.

I shrieked again when I realized how high we were, then quickly shut my eyes again. I started praying, alternating between whispering the Our Father and the Hail Mary. I leaned forward so my father could hear me, and quietly asked, "Please drive slower, don't drive us over the cliff, I don't want to be eaten by a vulture."

It was terrifying at every curve, and I kept repeating my prayers over and over, until my mother snapped, "Ya cállate, shut up, you're making me nervous," she said as she pulled me in close to lean on her.

I often think about my mom and admire how she raised seven children, always having breakfast, lunch, and dinner ready for us. Even if it was only rice and beans, she still managed to make a dessert of a fried flour tortilla with cinnamon sugar on top. We were delighted with our meals. I often hear her voice saying to me when I was a teen, "Dela, comb your hair y ponte un lipstick." Both Mom and Dad encouraged us to look nice.

I had fallen asleep when we reached a point where our side of the road had crumbled away so severely that we couldn't pass. I woke up hearing everyone's commentary. There was a massive gap in the road as if a boulder had tumbled down the mountainside, knocking off a chunk of the roadway. We waited patiently as we watched a car approaching from the opposite side. Carefully, the car passed at a snail's pace, moving forward and hugging the mountainside, trying not to scrape their car against the jagged rocks. We then did the same, skirting around our eroded path. I kept praying that another chunk of the road wouldn't collapse while we were crossing.

Once we reached the last stretch of the winding road, we finally felt at ease. After all the chatter about how dangerous it was, my brother Joe started asking about the ranch and what the plan was. My father hadn't shared much with us before we left—after all, we were just kids—but now he shared that we would arrive at his sister's home, and after a week, he would return to work at the steel mill to finish the year. He explained that we could go to the ranch once we were ready to adjust to living outside the city. He mentioned that there was a horse at the ranch, and we would sleep in hammocks. He also shared that there were plenty of fruits, such as mangos, bananas, and coconuts, that grew on the property for sale. We were all young, so it all sounded like a great big, exciting adventure. We were going to live on a ranch in Mexico, where we would have plenty of fruit and a horse.

The only one born in Mexico was my father. The rest of us were born in the U.S. —my siblings and I in Texas, and the younger half of the family in Indiana. Even my mother was born in Pennsylvania. Her father, a Mexican immigrant, had moved north with his wife to work at a steel mill in Coatesville just before the Great Depression of 1929.

So, aside from my father, we would all be foreigners living in Mexico.

My mother always went along with my father's decisions — the old-school macho dynamic ruled our household. We didn't get a say in where we lived or what came next. But we were young, and we were just excited that we had a horse waiting to greet us.

My brother Joe, who was fourteen, asked, "What color is the horse?"

"White," my father said.

Sylvia, who was twelve, was sitting behind the driver's side with her head practically hanging out of the window, trying to keep cool, when she quickly pulled in and looked over at me. She heard "white horse" and probably imagined riding it every day to the nearby beach that my father had mentioned. My thought was, *Okay, that sounds nice . . . if we can safely make it down this mountain.* I kept praying and kept my eyes closed, peeking every now and then until we finally made it down to a very nice surprise.

We arrived to find a midsize pool formed from a waterfall that cascaded down the mountain. It was a natural park—no parking lot, no bathrooms, no guards—just nature giving us a reprieve from the scare and the heat. It was a perfect spot to swim. The waterfall was gentle and poured down over some large, flat boulders. My brother climbed up the side of the mountain and then jumped into the rolling water, sliding down the rocks' smooth surface, spilling into the pool. My sister and father did the same, as Jesse and I stood in the water watching them. My mother was napping with the young ones on a blanket in the grass. It was a delightful moment after such a terrifying ride. Before long we were back on the road to Villahermosa, now only a few hours away. And yes, it was even hotter now that we were closer to sea level, but we were not quite at the sea yet.

VILLAHERMOSA, TABASCO

Arriving at Villahermosa was a beautiful sight as we rolled down the street alongside the Grijalva Riverbank. The pretty pink flowers of the trumpet trees lined the road as we passed a horse here and there, with its master in a battered straw hat leading the way. We stopped to buy refreshments, as alluring, perfumed couples, freshly dressed after their siesta and shower, now strolled or sat on park benches and at tables in the plazas. They sipped Coca-Cola or limeade, listening to romantic bolero music played by strolling musicians who strummed guitars as a soloist bounced mallets on a wooden marimba. We also listened to the music as we sipped our refreshments before returning to the car to drive into the neighborhood where my father's sister,

Consuelo, lived. She was married to a poet whose tribute to the beautiful city was the city's official poem.

When we arrived after a long car trip with no air conditioning, you can imagine how eager we all were to shower and how ready we were for our assigned beds. In this case, it was a lukewarm shower and a hammock to catch up on our sleep and de-stress from the adventure we had just experienced. If you have never slept in a hammock, it has two advantages. First, the rocking back and forth soothes you to sleep, and the other is the breeze it creates. The breeze, along with a wet washcloth over your face, can be the next best thing to keeping cool, just long enough to fall asleep.

The next day, we were expecting to go to the ranch, but Dad said, "Let's visit with family first," and decided we would go the following day since Consuelo, our hostess, and my mom were up early with plans to make chicken with red chile mole (moh-leh) sauce for dinner.

Making mole is a long process that starts with going to the market to buy the live chicken, the *chile ancho*, and not to forget the sesame seeds and queso fresco—the fresh cheese that crumbles so nicely on top of the enchiladas that you can make with leftover chicken mole. That was the original recipe for enchiladas. There wasn't any American cheese or sour cream in Mexican food back then.

I was walking into the kitchen just in time to see my aunt grab the chicken by the throat, swing it around her head, break its neck, and throw it down to the ceramic floor. I screamed! I had no idea that was how you killed a chicken for your dinner. With the lack of refrigeration, people would shop for their daily meals in the early mornings. My aunt did have a refrigerator, but none of the kids were allowed to open the door. We had to ask an adult. They guarded it like a safe. We were told that neighbors would buy ice or ask to store a food item, so they didn't want anything to go missing, melt, or spoil.

The aroma of the toasted sesame seeds made us hungry and anxious to sit and finally eat. We had a delicious home-cooked dinner, complete with sliced avocados and ice-cold Coca-Cola or limeade—my favorite—made from the lime tree in the back yard. With everyone sitting at the dinner table, it was time to catch up with the family, especially our sister Sally. She was a year and a half younger than I and had been raised by my aunt since she was a young baby. My aunt, who had already raised an adopted child, was now raising my sister. She had asked my dad to allow her to raise Sally, since she had not been able to conceive her own child. My mother, always following my father's decisions, had no say in it. I don't believe my father intended to leave her in Mexico forever, even after a couple of attempts to motivate her to stay when visiting our home in Indiana. I can't blame her for not wanting to stay with seven siblings who didn't speak the same language. She didn't want to partake in any of the chores Sylvia, and I had planned for her. It was so inexpensive in Mexico to have a woman come into your home to clean, shop, and do the laundry. Today, it may cost more, but it's still part of the culture. So, she was not doing chores. Nor did she want to attend an American school. Her life was much more pleasant in Mexico, being the only child. No chores for her and no American name—her name is Celia.

EL RANCHO

The next morning after breakfast, the women were in the kitchen preparing food to bring on our trip to check out the ranch. We were all excited as we piled into the car, squeezing my aunt and sister Celia into the station wagon. I had to sit in the back section with my legs folded up, along with my brother Jesse. The ranch was about eighteen miles outside of the city limits. Once off the main paved road, we turned onto a dry and very dusty dirt road in a lush and fertile region. We had to close all of the windows because of all the dust. I could still see the road, which was lined with trees of all sorts and sizes, including rubber trees, banana trees, coconut palms, and other various palm trees. Occasionally, a colorful red hibiscus plant would add real beauty to the dusty road, ready for picking its abundant flowers to dry and make 'Agua de Jamaica' or hibiscus tea. I like it with crushed mint leaves and a squirt of lime; no sugar for me.

Our two male cousins, who were the caretakers of the property, greeted us when we arrived. Their father, my dad's brother, lived nearby, and they would harvest the mangos, coconuts, papayas, limes, and sour oranges to sell at the market. With no electricity in the area, they had been expecting us because of the letter my father had sent to notify them that we were coming. They were surprised but happy to see us. Right away, our cousins offered to bring down some coconuts to drink and sweet mangos to eat. You could smell the sweetness in the hot, humid air.

While my brother Joe and sister Sylvia got to take turns riding the old horse, I turned and walked away with my mother as I saw my sister's disappointed face when we learned that it was merely a grey horse that now had white hair from aging.

I was in shock, and Jesse seemed equally surprised as we walked into the house with my mother. It wasn't a house but a hut with a thatched roof made of dried palm leaves called palapa. The walls were woven from the fibers of the local trees and plants available, allowing ventilation from any breeze to flow through. There was a hardwood sink and a hand pump to bring up water from the well. A clay oven was still warm, with a heavy cast-iron comal and a leftover tortilla still on the griddle. Lying against a wooden rack for keeping food supplies were a couple of old, used machetes, likely used to cut down the banana stalks of short, plump bananas. I looked around the rest of the bare hut, which only contained a few hammocks and a couple of baskets with clothes and towels. A table sat in the center, with a few wooden chairs on the hard-packed, smooth dirt floor. While my siblings were playing outside, I spun around, thinking, *something's not right. This can't be what my father had planned for us to live in.*

When I stepped back outside, my cousins were showing my dad and brother the cacao plants, the sour orange trees, the banana trees, and my father's favorite fruit, the papaya. As Jesse and I walked around the outside of the hut, we were stunned to find a huge hog lying in his pen. We were told they were fattening him up to take him to market soon. I wondered how they were going to move that huge animal.

Before long, the day's adventure was over. My mother suggested we leave before the mosquitoes came out of their hiding places, as the afternoon was dying down.

Heading home, we were all sweaty and dusty and all talked about how we could never live in a hut. My father didn't have much to say until his week was over. He kissed us all goodbye, telling us where to find a place to live and get registered for school, and that he'd be back in time for Christmas.

RETURNING TO THE STATES

As soon as my dad left, my brother Joe told my mother we could only stay until it was time to get back to school in September. She agreed. She didn't like the idea of living in Mexico for many reasons that affected us kids. First, it was about the differences in the food. Back home, we would have pancakes with Log Cabin syrup, but all we could find was Karo corn syrup or very dark, thick molasses, so none of us wanted the pancakes she made. We loved our Corn Flakes, but we couldn't stand to drink the raw milk that was not homogenized, so no cereal. There were no buns for our hamburgers, nor was there Heinz ketchup or sliced pickles. Perhaps you could find these products in Mexico City, but Villahermosa was still a small town with limited demand for our staples. We were too Americanized and yearned for food we were accustomed to.

My mother wasn't keen on buying a live chicken only to have to bring it home to do the 'swing the chicken over your head' dance to crack the neck. She would then have to pluck the feathers and then run it over an open flame to remove whatever feathers were too slippery to pull. Nope, my mother wasn't going through all that. One thing for sure was that she made a lot of tacos with hamburger meat and plenty of avocado, or scrambled eggs with potatoes, and our staple of rice and beans accompanied by plenty of ice-cold Coca-Cola that came in the big thirty-two-ounce glass bottles. Occasionally, Consuelo would cook a chicken.

Mom started saving every penny she could from the money my father gave her as well as the money he sent after he left. She never mentioned to my dad that we would be returning in time for the start of the fall semester of school. When she realized it was not enough for the bus tickets for all of us, she asked Grandpa back in Texas to help us out. As soon as she received the money, she bought the tickets. We were all so ready to leave because, as young Americans, we couldn't even see our favorite cartoons on TV like *The Flintstones, The Jetsons, Mister Magoo,* or *Quick Draw McGraw,* which was my sister Sylvia's favorite.

The day finally came when we were ready to leave. It was mid-August, and tickets were purchased for our first leg from Villahermosa to Mexico City. We said our goodbyes, hugged our sister Celia goodbye, and off we went on our way back to the States. The bus was brand new with air conditioning and was very comfortable. It was the first cool air we had experienced since leaving Indiana. The bus left in the evening and arrived by morning. We then had to take the second bus to Monterey, crossing the mountains, and this time I wasn't paying attention. This bus was an old one with no air conditioning. I must have slept most of the way because I don't recall much, but I do remember when we were in the bus station in Monterey. My brother was sent to buy tickets for the final bus ride to the border. Again, it was an old bus with no air conditioning. Again, I don't remember the trip until we arrived at the Reynosa border. We all got off the bus and walked across the bridge to the American Border Patrol officers' stations, where a smiling officer asked us, "Is everyone here American?"

We all happily shouted, "Yes!"

We were so glad we had made it back safely.

The next friendly face was that of my smiling grandpa standing on US soil. He stood tall, wearing his well-worn fedora hat, khaki pants, and shirt. He always looked like the farm foreman he had been for many years, driving his truck with his family and other workers around the United States during harvest time after the Depression. He then opened a saloon—Rocha's Place—complete with a red Coca-Cola cooler and a waitress wearing a big, wide Mexican skirt with the sparkling design of a Mexican town with wooden houses, a salon, and vaqueros with their horses. We all ran to him and hugged him until he said, "Okay, okay, get in the truck. Grandma is waiting."

As we headed home to Elsa, he asked, "What do you want from the store before we get home?"

We all shouted, "Milk!"

Learn the history of your family, your language, and your culture.
It will make you a more interesting and confident person.

CHAPTER 2

Arrival to New York City

I was still a senior in high school in East Chicago, Indiana, when I started working as a dance teacher at the Fred Astaire Dance Studio in downtown Chicago. Attending summer school to earn extra credits cleared the path for a light senior class schedule, which required only two classes to graduate. Right after class ended at 11:00 a.m., I would quickly go home, change clothes, and grab the lunch my mom had prepared. I would then drive myself to the South Shore station to catch a train heading north, ready to start work by 2:00 p.m.

It was all very exciting as a seventeen-year-old to travel into downtown Chicago five days a week. I could get dressed up, wear my high heels and makeup, and walk to work from the nearby train station. There was no college for me at the time. When I asked my mother for the twelve dollars for the SAT test, she said, "No, we don't have any money to send you to college," adding, "Don't worry, you'll find a job."

Well, I did. As I walked the few blocks to my job, I'd window shop and wander into one of my favorite shoe shops to see what was on the sales rack. I was always on the lookout for beautiful shoes I could afford.

Before arriving at the dance studio, I would read the many billboards on State Street, which was then known as a theater hub. I recall the day it read on a music theater marquee: "STEVIE WONDER TONIGHT." I got excited and didn't think twice. I had a few dollars, which I counted and found that I had just enough money to buy the ticket if I skipped buying my dinner snack for the return trip home at the end of the day. I already had my weekly train pass to get home.

I bought my first concert ticket and felt perfectly fine about going by myself. I was already independent at seventeen, and I was used to traveling alone. It was safe back then, for the most part. It was Friday night, but I worked until 9:00 p.m. I slipped out of work to get to the concert, which had started already. As I got closer, I could already hear the music and then the singing as I opened the door. I walked in and found a seat in the back rows because the main floor was full. The audience was singing along with Stevie, so I joined the mostly standing crowd, singing, "For Once in my Life," then "Signed, Sealed, Delivered I'm Yours." The experience left me with a burning desire to be on stage. I envisioned myself surrounded by the enthusiastic audience, with the fine musicians all playing behind me while I sang under the warmth of the changing red, blue, and white spotlight.

I was no stranger to the stage. I had played violin since grade school, and in high school, I was also one of the Madrigal Singers who got to perform in a couple of events, opening for music acts coming to perform in Gary, Indiana. We moved a lot, which is how I got to meet Ramsey Lewis and Deniece Williams ("Let's Hear It for the Boy"), who being coached by our music teachers at the first Martin Luther King High School in Gary. I got to play "Pomp and Circumstance" about a hundred times while my sister Sylvia and all the graduates walked in to take a seat for their commencement program. For my sister's school graduation party, Michael Jackson and the Jackson 5 performed, which was likely one of their early gigs, as she mentioned he was around five years old at the time. Lucky her.

Music was all around where I lived. We could hear the singing coming out of the many Baptist churches in my neighborhood in Calumet before moving to Gary. Like I said, we moved around a lot. There was even a record shop on my block with its outside speakers playing the best rhythm and blues, like Lou Rawls or King Pleasure, as well as lots of soul music, such as Aretha Franklin's, and early Motown hits like "Please Mr. Postman" by the Marvelettes and "Shop Around" by The Miracles.

Once a month, at the dance studio, we would host a Friday night dance for our students, and we would also feature a special event for members of the "Golden Dancers Club." I got to see Tony Bennett perform with his band for the first time at the London House in Chicago. It was a fine, elegant dining room with a grand piano on stage, accompanied by two rows of musicians dressed in black tuxedos and black bow ties. The high ceiling was decorated with sparkling chandeliers. The waiters, in white gloves, brought our dinner plates and small dishes, including one with a halved lemon wrapped in an elastic-edged cheesecloth cover to catch the seeds. It was also the first time I had so many forks to use. My student said, "Just start from the outside and work in."

When the show was over, I quickly jumped up from my table to move in close and shake Mr. Bennett's hand, and then I didn't want to let it go. I was floating in heaven all the way home.

The next outing was for the annual autumn dance competition in New York City (NYC). I felt incredibly fortunate to have a student sign up for the trip.

We would be joining the nine dancing couples competing. Living in a small apartment on the Near North Side of Chicago and being not quite eighteen, I had to get permission from my parents. It was weeks before my birthday, and there I was on a plane to the Big Apple.

The trip was only for three nights. When we arrived, the cab driver asked if we wanted the tourist tour to the hotel. I said, "Of course!"

The drive from LaGuardia Airport took us over the Triboro Bridge, now called the Robert F. Kennedy Bridge, and through Harlem, passing right by the Apollo Theater on 125th Street. I couldn't believe the number of people filling the sidewalks and spilling into the street like it was a street fair, but the cab driver said, "No, it's like this all the time—people like to party outdoors to see their friends because apartments are too small. Additionally, October in New York City is an ideal time of year, with the weather just right. Just lock the doors back there."

We rode down Broadway past Manhattan School of Music, Barnard, and Columbia University, past the 96th Street subway station and all the many shops. Then we drove past Lincoln Center and down to the hotel just before Times Square. I quickly dropped off my luggage in my room, headed back down the elevator, and out to the street. As I walked on 7th Avenue away from the Sheraton Hotel where we stayed, I could see blinking lights.

It was 1972, one month before my eighteenth birthday, and I felt lucky to be walking toward Times Square, surrounded by its billboards for Coca-Cola, Kodak, Camel Cigarettes, and Budweiser, among others. Then there were the marquees of the theatres, all lit up with the many musicals and plays.

Strolling was easy with no crowds of people and light car traffic. You could find a parking spot or cross the street without the feeling of being crushed by a mob or run over by a car or an e-bike, as you often do today. Annual tourism in New York at that time was only 8 to 9 million for the year, compared to

61 million in 2023, according to the city's visitors bureau. Yes, I was lucky to be strolling, admiring all the billboards while sipping an Orange Julius. It all left such a significant impression on me that I said, "I'm coming back!"

When we returned, I couldn't stop talking about New York City to my co-workers. Here I thought Chicago was special, but the Big Apple was even more special. One of the girls I worked with said, "Enough already with New York. Let's go to this nightclub where my boyfriend is the doorman." She assured me that he would let us in since we were underage.

Just as she said, he let us in, and within minutes we were dancing to the great band that was playing. Angelina kept looking at the front door until she saw her boyfriend in the club and walked into the musicians' dressing room. She quickly said, "Come on, let's go to the bathroom because we have to pass the dressing room where the guys are."

As we casually walked, she grabbed my arm and pushed me into the dressing room's curtain, then followed me and promptly went up to her guy, starting a conversation.

There I was, standing quietly, as I suddenly locked eyes with a tall, fine-looking musician. He had long hair, a goatee, and a smile revealing a single dimple. Gently, he leaned forward, placing his hand under my chin and giving me a tender kiss on the lips. I melted in my shoes.

We talked a bit, and I asked where he was from—I hadn't met anyone who resembled his stature before. He said he was from Argentina. The only thing I knew about Argentina was that it was in South America—nothing more.

The short break time was over, but he managed to jot down my number in a book of matches. Two weeks later, he called to ask me out on our first date. Six months later, we were married. Being the gifted musician he was, he declared that we would be moving to New York City to further his musical career.

By October 1973, I was back in the Big Apple, married to Jorge Dalto. On our first night out, we went to see Eddie Palmieri at Carnegie Hall. It was packed with screaming fans all around. Salsa was still new to my ears; my musical preferences at the time were Santana, El Chicano, and the Motown sound—music that lit up my Mexican American/Chicana soul.

As a dance teacher, I did dance mambo and cha-cha, and salsa was just beginning to gain popularity with the Fania sound produced by the new record label. That night, I became a fan indeed.

After the show, we went down to the Village Gate nightclub to hear the Thad Jones and Mel Lewis orchestra—an iconic jazz band whose surviving members still perform there, in one of the longest-surviving jazz clubs.

We eventually made our way to an underground spot, where our new friends, Julie Janeiro and Tito Russo, were playing hot Brazilian samba music—music I wasn't very familiar with at the time. Julie stood on a wooden box for the stage, her shiny microphone in hand, wearing a sexy red fishnet rhinestone top and tight leather pants. I'm sure she had even the mice behind the walls dancing samba.

It was a great time for music in Greenwich Village, with numerous affordable music clubs that stayed open until 4:00 a.m., fueling the city that never sleeps.

Every night was an adventure. The city was alive with artists of all kinds, and with so many venues, you could run into someone interesting in a restaurant, a nightclub, or even on the street.

One day, while walking down Fifth Avenue to hail a cab, I spotted Mickey Rooney standing with his bodyguard. When I realized it was him, I said, "Go ahead, you can take this one."

He gave me a great big smile and said, "Thank you, babe."

I stood there for a moment in awe—he called me *babe*! I couldn't help but think, *Wow, who am I going to run into next?*

Of all the many types of personalities, some were good, while others were not so good. It was a bit dangerous in those days. Car alarms would sound off every night from car thefts, with thieves stealing the cassette players. One night, coming home from a club in the middle of winter, I thought out my one-block walk home. The parking garage was located across the street from a single-room occupancy hotel where some shady individuals resided. I was wearing my fur coat, carrying my purse, and holding a cloth bag with a liquor bottle that someone had given me, as it was holiday time. It was a frigid and windy night, and it was 3:00 a.m. I thought, *what idiot thief would be out working in this weather?* I only had to cross Amsterdam Avenue, past the corner high-rise, and then walk past the first brownstone to get to my building. It was four steps down to the building doorway, then into the small hall and the locked second door. I thought, *now move quickly before anyone can see me leave the garage.* I made my way to the corner, dashing across the street. *Just a few more long strides*, I told myself, *then down the steps and into my building.*

I thought, *I'm safe.* I rang the doorbell so my husband could open the locked door into the main hall. As I turned to lean on the entrance door, two young men jumped down the stairs and kicked the door so hard that it swung open, with me crashing against the brick wall. I started screaming, then felt the wet, warm stream running down my leg. One guy quickly grabbed my purse, and while the other one struggled to grab the liquor bag on the floor. As he stood up, he grabbed my lapel and felt the fur. It was a white mink with beautiful black accents down the sleeves. It was a gorgeous twenty-eighth birthday present, and I certainly wasn't giving it up without a struggle. However, I believe he didn't know what it was or its value at the time. He just faced me with his big brown eyes and dropped jaw. Just then, my husband emerged half asleep, brandishing a machete he had grabbed as he heard my screaming as they ran off.

I immediately called the police, and they were there in seconds. They said they had been making the rounds because of other troubles in the area with the arrival of the Marielitos, a name used to identify the newly arrived Cubans that Fidel Castro had released, after being incarcerated in Cuba. After the police left with their report, I realized I had wet myself from the shock.

I was traumatized by this incident for several years. If I were walking down the street, I would always look back to see if anyone was around. If someone was following me, I was told to cross the street, and if the person was still following me, I was to then run to the nearest business or a building with a doorman. One of my Brazilian friends, who worked as a waitress and walked home after her late shift, said she always carried a cup of hot coffee as a weapon. I decided to buy some pepper spray instead, and thankfully, I never had to use it. Eventually, the city got better, and you could hear the difference, with fewer annoying car alarms.

Just the same, I was glad I lived in New York City. When we first arrived, Jorge suggested that I take singing lessons, as I was always singing the lyrics of popular songs. The lessons came in handy when the arranger/conductor Chico O'Farrell called me for my first commercial. It was a fortunate opportunity, as one of his regular Latina singers was unavailable. After the recording, Chico said, "Now go join the union and take some solfege lessons with Maestro Alberto Socarras."

Maestro Socarras was a Cuban flutist who arrived in NYC around 1924. He was one of the first Cubans to work and perform at the Apollo Theater. He showed me a picture of the marquee that read, "Alberto Socarras and his Magic Flute." He had an excellent career writing arrangements for Cab Calloway and other artists of that time. He may have recorded one of the first flute solos ever, according to recent research by Cuban Prof. Janio Abrea for his thesis.

I was now a member of the American Federation of Television and Radio Artists (AFTRA) and the Screen Actors Guild (SAG), the union for singing commercials and working in films. One of several commercials was with Ray Charles singing "America." However, the opportunity to sing as a backup singer for Celia Cruz at Madison Square Garden was one of the many exciting early highlights I experienced. To this day, I can still feel the excitement of the packed arena. And when I say packed, I mean twenty thousand Fania Records salsa fans in the audience. As I walked up the stairs and onto the stage, I could feel the warmth of all those voices roaring down from the furthest rows. I looked out, but all I could see were the rays of hundreds of colorful lights, sending heat and an overwhelming force. The sound grew stronger, like a barricade pushing against me. The lights were so bright that I could only see people sitting out in the first ten rows or so.

When Celia stepped onto the stage, the wall of roaring fans only got louder. The hair stood up on my arms. As she began to sing, I couldn't believe I was standing there behind Celia, on the Madison Square Garden stage, at twenty-two, and as a Chicana singing Salsa. However, by then, I had become a professional singer. If I could stay in tune, read music, and have a good even tempo, I would be hired. There wasn't a Chicano or a Mexican population when I first arrived, so jazz, Salsa, and Brazilian was the music in demand that I chose to learn.

The difference between jazz, salsa, Afro-Cuban, Brazilian, Cumbia, and any other Latin American music lies in understanding the clavé (pronounced *cla-vé*) rhythm of the piece of music. By "*clavé*," I mean the placement of the accents that identifies the style of music. For dancers, if it isn't in clavé, they can't dance to it because the accents won't sync with the steps. I also had the advantage of being able to speak English, Spanish, and Brazilian Portuguese, and learned to sing in clavé, which helped me get the many calls to perform.

The gigs were great, but they didn't offer health insurance, so there were times when I had to get a day job for the benefits. By this time, I had two children. Jorge was always traveling with the jazz guitarist George Benson around the world, and many other artists that would call him to record a solo, hoping it would help earn them a Grammy Award. I landed a job to be an assistant to Jane Henson of the Muppets. It turned out to be a fun job, with the opportunity to take my boys to watch Jim Henson and Frank Oz rehearsing Kermit the Frog and Miss Piggy and visiting the workshop where the many puppets for *Sesame Street* were being built.

At one of the after parties from an event, I got to sit next to Anthony Quinn. I was so starstruck I wouldn't leave his side, convinced he would ask me to marry him. Unfortunately, he was already married. Oh, and so was I.

I had several jobs at different times when the traveling gigs were slow. However, I would quit my day job when the local gigs picked up or when I received an offer to travel somewhere to perform. The best deal was when I could stay home and work locally, allowing me to be near my family. One summer, I was working eight gigs in seven days. I had a steady gig at the beautiful Rainbow Room with its revolving dance floor at the top of Rockefeller Center, which was very popular. This was during the dot-com boom, and it seemed like money was in every conversation heard coming in and out of restaurants, on dance floors, in elevators, or when people talked into cell phones while waiting for a cab.

People were making money and coming out to spend it. Musicians had plenty of work, from packed clubs to private events at beach houses and on private yachts. I was lucky to have my steady gig at the Rainbow Room, where our work sometimes extended to seven performances a week. People booked weddings, birthdays, and corporate parties, where we performed to encourage dancing. One evening, James Brown came in to have dinner and dance with his wife as a show of good faith, after his wife had dropped charges accusing him of domestic violence, which had made it to the news.

The eighth gig of the week took place at the coffee shop across from Union Square Park, near the popular farmer's market. It was a bustling corner. Our friends and fans would come, some bringing their kids to have lunch, while I'd sing about fifty Brazilian songs before rushing off to my next stage at the Rainbow Room.

Being a singer and a mom was not easy—then again, it's not easy for any working mom. I was raising the babies while Jorge was on the road working intensely for years, rehearsing and directing George Benson's band with only layovers at home before continuing on tour. Jorge was the musical director when many of those shows included a string orchestra, thanks to the award-winning recording of *Breezin'*, featuring Jorge's unforgettable piano solo on the platinum hit "This Masquerade."

Jorge worked constantly—until a tumor appeared and was diagnosed as cancer. Everything came to a stop. After rounds of chemotherapy failed to help, I had to face the terrible day when I broke the news to the boys that he would not survive.

It's a pain we will always carry. When you lose someone you love so deeply, it feels like a piece of your heart was carved out, and in sharing this with you it has brought tears again after so many years. The pain never goes away and yet we must carry on.

Yes, and now as a single mom, it was not easy. But the three of us learned to support each other. Not a day goes by without a memory being stirred—by me, someone in the family, or the many friends and fans who still speak of the beauty Jorge created with his hands on the piano.

My days became a blur of responsibility and quiet determination. I started each morning getting the boys off to school, tidying up the house, thinking about what to cook—if I had time—while practicing lyrics for a new song. I'd make calls to book gigs, help with the boys' homework, then head out to rehearsals or shows.

I remember calling out as I rushed out the door, "Order some food, the money is in the box," then pausing to look at them and adding, "Please, do the right thing."

My oldest would sometimes demand, "But we want real food."

I'd have to promise to cook chicken soup or Milanesa cutlets the next day. I'd ask if they wanted a babysitter, and they'd insist, "No, we have a doorman, we don't need a babysitter."

My boys learned to take care of themselves with the help from Dina, their godmother and her son Nando, or my brother Jesse and a wink from the doorman as I left the building.

It was the time of the Atari 500, so the boys stayed home most of the time or played sports. Then the Apple computer came along, and it really absorbed them with making beats. That was the hook—I didn't have to worry about them. They'd bring their friends over to work on making music. Little did I know that they would help themselves to the cash I left in the little wooden jewelry box for food or emergencies, using it to buy subway passes to head to the Grand Arcade spot in Times Square. It wasn't until years later, at our Thanksgiving dinners, when we'd share stories and laugh a lot, that they confessed how they used to skip school to go to the arcade.

Life in New York City felt like an adventure every single day—you never knew what you might encounter. One moment, you'd see Paul Simon casually crossing the street, and the next, you'd be looking up at a helicopter circling overhead, searching for a thief in the neighborhood.

Another day, it could be a citywide blackout, with flickering candles lighting up building entrances and people stuck in elevators, waiting for the power to return.

You might find yourself watching the Macy's Thanksgiving Day Parade balloons being blown up the night before their grand procession down Fifth Avenue. Or hopping on the Staten Island Ferry for a free ride across the bay, saluting the Statue of Liberty as she stood tall against the skyline.

A stroll through Central Park could lead you to a free classical concert, a hip-hop show, a pop singer belting out tunes, or the rumba players heating up the lawn by the park's lake.

There was never a boring day. All you had to do was step outside, and adventure was waiting.

When life brings you challenge, hope, and heartbreak—
face it with courage and carry on.

CHAPTER 3

Barbeque and a Military Coup

was six months pregnant when we arrived at the airport in Argentina. As soon as we stepped out of the immigration corridor, I saw happy hands of various sizes waving and heard loud, excited voices shouting, "Jorge, Adela, acá, acá," ("Over here, over here!")

I saw about twenty-five people all smiling, gleefully shouting out our names, running up to us with bright, colorful flowers, and wrapping us in hugs and kisses. The group included Jorge's parents, his aunts, his sister and brother, and a lively mix of the in-laws, cousins, nieces, and nephews who traveled to the airport from Roque Perez and Hurlingham—towns outside of Buenos Aires.

Then there were the musicians who had driven in from Buenos Aires to greet Jorge and his wife, whom everyone was meeting for the first time.

I was overwhelmed by so many kisses and smiles, especially after the long fourteen-hour flight. I could already feel the baby inside me giving a little kick now and then, probably wondering, *What the heck is all the commotion?*

Finally, everyone followed us outside the airport to get into cars for the ride to Roque Pérez, the small town where Jorge was born and where a large part of the extended family and friends lived. We were on our way to the *asado* they had planned for us. I heard so much about how great an authentic Argentine barbeque could be that I was looking forward to the meal.

Juan Carlos, my brother-in-law, led the way to the parking lot, but suddenly, I stopped just a few steps outside the airport. I was stunned to see soldiers stationed around the entrance with machine guns in their hands.

Before I could say anything, Jorge grabbed me by the arm and said, "Keep walking."

It was the fall of 1976, and we arrived several months after Argentina had experienced a military coup that overthrew the government of President Isabel Perón, the second widow of the former president Juan Perón. Once we were in the car, Juan Carlos explained that the military was now in control of the government and that we had to always carry our passports. Additionally, we could expect to be stopped at any time and would have to show our identification.

He also cautioned us to be mindful of what we said—and to whom. The military was cracking down, aggressively hunting for left-wing guerrilla groups in the name of restoring order. But in reality, it was the beginning of a dark period under a military dictatorship that would last until 1983.

I thought about our appearance. Jorge had long hair and a goatee, and we looked like hippies with our bell-bottom jeans. We hadn't seen soldiers with machine guns in any of our travels in the US, so it was unnerving. Within a few miles, we hit the first roadblock on the highway. We rolled down the windows so the soldiers could see our faces and check our passports before waving us through. It felt uneasy for all of us in the car until we arrived at the small cattle town north of Buenos Aires. The townsfolk of Roque Perez were waiting to greet Jorge, the renowned pianist who had moved to the United States and was now returning home after several years.

Again, I was surrounded by more family and friends. Faces of all ages—from the most wrinkled of the elders with their curious expressions, caressing my face and arms, and even a pinch on my butt like an Italian initiation from my father-in-law, to the most tender of faces by young, smiling cousins surrounding me, the new addition to the family with child.

By then, I had forgotten about the military coup and was preoccupied with food. I saw the gaucho-dressed head cook at the grill, using his shiny steel wood poker to check the burning logs. The aroma was inviting, with meat sizzling on the long flat grill, filled with so many parts of a cow, you could taste it in the air. They were fat steaks and beef ribs to make your mouth water. Then the *achuras*—like sweetbreads, braided intestines, livers, kidneys, and even the *criadillas* (bull testicles) for the most macho of the men. While we waited for the meats, a tray filled with chicken, cheese, and beef empanadas was passed around, followed by a tray of blood sausages and Argentine chorizos, a sausage they place on a football roll and smothered with chimichurri, the zesty, herbaceous chimichurri—the sauce made of chopped parsley, a tiny dash of crushed red pepper flakes, salt, garlic, red vinegar, and the best olive oil.

We all sat at a couple of long tables where everyone was talking, laughing, and eating. The tables were set with glasses of red wine and loaves of warm Italian bread, sliced at an angle. Yes, there was also a salad of lettuce and delicious tomatoes, cut in chunks with olive oil, salt, and red wine vinegar. One could be happy just dunking the warm, fresh bread into the sauces on any of the platters that swept past our eyes. The most delicious-looking free-range chicken was also on the grill, with the skin turning a nice, crispy brown, which turned out to be my favorite.

What a feast it was, and I was amazed to hear that the *asado* didn't require a special event, holiday, or celebration. It was the way to cook the abundance of great-tasting beef and to share the love by sitting with family and friends who often gathered in the small town. They also shared their love by sipping green *maté* tea from a gourd with a metal straw, which sat comfortably in your palm. It would be passed from hand to hand around the table, with the hot water pot never allowed to cool.

They also make a delicious caramel from the rich cow's milk, called *dulce de leche,* by cooking the milk down to a thick caramel. It's eaten by the spoonful, or in crepes, or within attractive petit fours called *macitas* filled or covered with *dulce de leche,* chocolate, or other delicious fillings, from fruits to nuts, that can't be beat anywhere in Latin America. Of course, the evening wouldn't have been complete without music. You could listen, dance, or sing along to tango being played with a bandoneon, which is an Italian-style accordion or concertina with buttons on each side of the instrument, along with another round of beef. Most of the men had their own personal steak knife, with elaborate silver or leather handles, used to pierce a cubed piece of beef from the final wooden board that was passed around to complete the feast, leaving everyone with happy bellies.

Argentina was fully colonized by the Spanish by 1580, establishing Spanish as the official language. Africans were brought over on Spanish ships as part of the transatlantic slave trade, contributing to the establishment of slavery in the region until slavery was abolished in 1813. By 1816, Argentina had gained its independence from Spain.

Cattle that arrived in ships to Panama as early as the 1700s gradually made their way south through the continent, thriving in the rich pampas grasslands of Argentina. This helped establish cattle ranching, with the *gaucho* cowboy playing a significant role in the country's economic growth.

Incoming waves of Europeans, particularly Italians before World War I, greatly influenced Argentine cuisine with their delicious pizzas, pastries, and pasta, as well as their renowned wines.

It took me a few days to recover from the feast, and before we left, I had a handful of recipes to add to my collection. Even with my belly growing a little more each day, I was in good shape to start my tour of the capital city, Buenos Aires, on our way to visit *El Teatro Globo*, the concert hall where we were scheduled to perform before our departure. I was a complete stranger to Argentina, knowing little about its history or culture, but I fell in love quickly.

As we drove around with my father-in-law in his small orange Citroën car, I was amazed at the city's vastness, with its grand mansions, government palaces, and institutional buildings. The elaborate facades, replicating the French Beaux-Arts and Italian Renaissance styles, were built in the nineteenth and twentieth centuries during the country's period of wealth and growth. When we walked, I felt as if I were strolling through the streets of Paris, passing wrought-iron gates and balconies, then walking through Parque Lezama. The park was designed by Charles Thays, a French-Argentine urbanist who was hired, with 90 percent of his drawings eventually used to design the city's gardens and parks, thereby completing the European flair. The Italian influence was represented by tall white columns, large planters under the tall, violet-flowered jacaranda trees that lined the parks, surrounded by cobblestone streets. Yes, I felt I was in Europe—even though I hadn't been there, yet.

I noticed women dressed in European styles, with a classy, upscale attitude, and the men were still using suits with ties while sitting at the cloth-covered tables in restaurants and cafes. As many people spilled out of the theaters, having just enjoyed live shows, waiters stood by, ready to attend to customers. They were dressed in their uniforms—a white shirt and black pants, with a white apron. Along with a cloth napkin draped over their left arm, used to present dishes, they also held a corkscrew, ready to open a bottle of their highly recommended Malbec red wine.

In the *botegón*, a no-frills café with wooden tables and chairs, the aroma could easily lure you in for a hearty meal of pasta, empanadas, or steak right off the grill, accompanied by a dish with a heaping scoop of creamy, delicious dulce de leche for dessert. You could walk in for *la hora del vermut*, or vermouth time. It's a traditional Argentine late afternoon snack, with a bottle of sweet vermouth and a soda siphon (or drink of your preference), accompanied with several petite dishes of cheese, crackers, olives, and any other tapas–style appetizers, as mouthwatering hams and garlic-smothered dishes. Tango music played Astor Piazzolla on a Victrola, or the voice of the heartthrob Carlos Gardel would fill the air; there was no denying you were in Argentina. No time to sit and enjoy leisure time? No problem. You can just go in to grab a slice of pizza from the abundant choices of the focaccia-style crust, or a quick espresso from the many stand-up coffee bars.

We shopped for clothes to blend in with the people, as the military could be seen in public, searching for left-wing guerrilla groups. We certainly didn't want to be wrongly identified as a member of anything other than The Jorge Dalto Interamerican Band, visiting family, and performing in Argentina.

Many people disappeared during *La Guerra Sucia* (The Dirty War, 1976-83), with possibly up to 30,000 left-wing political opponents, as well as civilians, intellectuals, and students who were marginally involved, who were captured and tortured, most of whom disappeared. It was *Las Madres de Plaza de Mayo*, the organized group of mothers formed in 1977, who identified themselves wearing white kerchiefs. Some were made from diapers, with the handwritten name of their missing beloved child. They carried their poster-sized pictures as they walked around the plaza across from the

Casa Rosada, the rose-colored government palace in downtown Buenos Aires. They became known around the world as they invited activists and advocates to speak on human rights and political causes. True heroines, such as Enriqueta Hernández de Narváez, aged one hundred, and Inés Rigo de Ragni, ninety-six, maintained their protest till their dying days. They were the last two remaining mothers and passed in September 2024, never knowing what happened to their children.

We continued moving through the city until we arrived at the historic Teatro del Global, a musical theater and music concert hall featuring grand French-style wooden doors and black and white tiles that lined the lobby floor. Jorge hadn't been home in five years, so we were expecting a full house, especially since he was the pianist for jazz guitarist George Benson, who had just earned a Grammy Award with Jorge's unforgettable piano solo, which Jorge had performed on the song "This Masquerade." It was exciting to be received at the theater. The greeter had a huge smile and assisted us with arranging all the details, from backstage logistics to the highest spotlight in the house. It was going to be a memorable concert, especially since I was carrying my baby bump onto the stage.

The following day, we continued our shopping and spotted the many gorgeous leather goods. There were plenty of boots in all styles and heights, from ankle-length shorties to over-the-knee, fine, hand-sewn boots. I found my pair of black boots with tall, quilted leather uppers that smoothly stretched over the shoe. I also fell in love with the many tourist souvenirs made of leather and silver, as well as hand-painted pottery. You can't leave the country without taking home your very own gourd to drink *maté* with the silver straw. If you're feeling indulgent, you might splurge on one with a gold-dipped mouthpiece. And, of course, you can't skip buying a handmade knife with a leather-wrapped handle, so that the next time a wooden tray of *asado* gets passed around, you can be ready to impale your sharp knife into a piece of meat that caught both your eye and your stomach's attention.

We were headed home to Hurlingham, where my father-in-law lived, as it was getting late after stopping for a 'portion' of pizza cut into hefty square servings. As we drove down an avenue behind an old city bus, I looked out the window, watching people walk with intention—stepping out of little shops, getting into their cars, and hopping into taxies, as shops began to dim their lights for the night. BAM! BAM! BAM! It sounded like staccato gunfire.

I recognized that sound as gunshots, and it scared me. I scrambled down to the floor of the little Citroen. There wasn't much room. As I looked up and out of the window, I saw someone being chased by a soldier, running across the roof of a row of one-story shops. My husband said, "Stay down!"

He explained that he'd seen the guy get out of the bus in front of us and somehow managed to climb onto the roof. We don't know what happened next because we certainly didn't stop to ask questions. We just kicked up our speed and headed straight home.

After that episode, we decided to limit our visits to Buenos Aires. We wanted to avoid any situation where we might be in the wrong place at the wrong time, especially with the military actively searching for people. So, instead of rehearsing in Buenos Aires, we scheduled the rehearsals closer to home.

We continued to have gatherings at our cousins' home in Roque Pérez a few more times. We had more *asado*, but also some tasty pasta dishes, including potato gnocchi in pesto sauce and eggplant stuffed ravioli in a chunky red tomato sauce. I listened to stories from the elder twins, Tia Lili and Tia Yoli, who filled me in about the Dalto family history. We took walks within the charming six-block radius of town, heading to the white-steepled church, and then continued to the cemetery to learn more about the history of the little town.

After almost four weeks of traveling, including a visit to the beach town of Mar del Plata to see family, who took us to observe the fur seals flopping around on the piers and sea lions sunbathing around the boat docks, we returned to Buenos Aires. It was showtime.

The house was packed, and the band was met with loud, explosive applause. The music, with its instrumental rhythmic sounds coming from Jorge's piano, followed by the bass, the drums, and the smooth slide of Alfredo Wulff's trombone, as the music rolled on. Finally, it was my turn. The applause was welcoming as I stepped onto the stage. I wore the black leather boots I had fallen in love with on my first day of shopping, with a black skirt and top, a colorful neck scarf, and my baby in my belly, now three weeks bigger. I suspect the applause was more out of sympathy for the vocalist with the baby belly when I took my bows.

After the show, we gathered at a restaurant near the 235-foot Obelisk, which stands tall, piercing the sky in the center of the Plaza de la República. Friends, fans, and musicians gathered in and outside the restaurant, where Jorge picked up the check, amazed at how affordable it was to eat such delicious food.

Before long, our trip was over. Around fifteen members of the family came to see us off, sending us home with a final gift from the shop at the airport that sells Alfajores. These sandwich cookies, featuring a dulce de leche filling, are dipped in chocolate or vanilla icing, making them a mouthwatering delight.

We checked in our overstuffed luggage, which contained new clothes, leather boots, the *maté* tea gourd, and hand-knit baby booties from the aunties. Now, we were headed home to safety, just weeks away from giving birth.

The important lesson I took from this trip was to always check the United States State Department website for information on the country you're visiting. You can find out if it's safe or at least know what to expect and the boundaries of safety. Let someone know where you're planning to visit and always leave your whereabouts with a couple of trusted people in case you run into trouble, which can happen anywhere in the world. But please, don't let that stop you from traveling—just inquire and plan accordingly.

I had the pleasure of returning to Argentina in 2014, when I remarried and introduced Robert to the family and the hospitality of Roque Pérez with its *asados*. We also visited Buenos Aires, which has grown immensely, but without the military presence. You still need to be cautious in your conversations, as you wouldn't want to risk being arrested for having the slightest connection with anyone who speaks out against the government. I'm not sure if it's still true today, but I wouldn't want to take the risk.

A very pleasurable moment in Buenos Aires is sitting in a sidewalk café, sipping a glass of Malbec, savoring a steak with chimichurri, and not forgetting that dollop of dulce de leche while listening to the music of Carlos Gardel.

CHAPTER FOUR

Ooh, la la, It's Paris!

had the opportunity to travel to France on two occasions. This particular trip was a birthday gift from Jorge—one of the most memorable presents I've ever received. I was turning twenty-eight, and life was treating us well. It was winter when he received a call to bring a band to Paris for a weeklong engagement to perform at The Château de Lombard, a new hot Salsa club on the music scene at the time. Jorge's popularity was growing after his Grammy® winning solo on Leon Russell's song "This Masquerade" recorded by George Benson. Calls were coming in with offers to travel with his group or with other artists. He was always very busy, not only traveling but also having recording dates with Chet Baker, Gato Barbieri, George Benson, Tito Puente, Carmen McRae, Dizzy Gillespie, Chico O'Farrill, Airto, Flora Purim, and Jerry Gonzalez, among others. He even performed with Julie Andrews for a concert at Radio City Hall in Rockefeller Center.

His schedule was so busy that I had to ask that he pencil me in his appointment book for a date. I was added to his calendar for Wednesdays, which was the slowest day of the week. The boys were four and five, so it meant calling a babysitter and making sure there was ice cream and a rented action movie to keep them distracted. They also wanted to spend time with their dad, so when I would be cooking, going out to do laundry, or shopping, Jorge would stay with them. We were lucky to have a backyard where we lived on West 95th street at that time, so they could have his undivided attention without wearing him down by having to go out of the home. We also managed to fit in a few vacations, sometimes joining Jorge at the end of a gig somewhere on the road. But we never got enough of Jorge's time—of fun, hugs, and kisses.

Jorge kept a busy schedule, and I managed the household and the boys. I had to ensure that all forty-six pairs of Jorge's socks were matched and that his stage clothes were prepared for any last-minute gigs with George Benson or a long tour that would last a few months. I would find time for myself once the boys were asleep. They had an 8:30 p.m. sleep schedule, which allowed me to tidy up before finally sitting down to have a little time for myself. My 'me time' was giving myself a manicure while memorizing or writing down new lyrics for a song that would jump out of me. I was always engaged in something related to music, whether it was practicing Solfege, learning a new song, or listening to other artists and their repertoire. Music was a constant in my life. I was recording vocals for commercials and performing in restaurants with cocktail lounges in the early stages of my career. Singing jazz standards with a Latin jazz rhythm and singing Brazilian songs, I learned to speak Portuguese. I had such a large selection of music charts that Jorge had written out for me in my key that I would say yes to any gig that would come my way; a corporate party, a Jewish wedding that wanted some Latin music to dance mambo, or a private party in East Hampton, as long as it was within my repertoire.

For the Paris gig, it required a full list of Salsa dance tunes, which wasn't for me. So, Ray De La Paz would be the singer, and for me, the trip would be my birthday present, along with a beautiful princess-cut white and black cross mink coat to wear in Paris. Besides, I was sure I would get invited to sing a couple of tunes—enough to satisfy my passion to perform.

The gig was for a week in December. I was thrilled to be going to Paris. I had been hoping to go one day to see the differences between France and Argentina.

The sixth member of the band, Carlos "Patato" Valdez, the Cuban conga player (RIP), was already in Paris. He was known around town as the little conga man with the tall French girlfriend. He met her while she played a conga on the street and was selling her handmade, fancy women's petit hats. The pair became inseparable.

Patato had a stunt where he would climb on top of his conga drums and tap dance for a few measures of music, then jump down to the stage floor in front of the drums. When I got to sing with the band, I would spot him in fear, thinking that one day he would lose his balance, but he never did. The audience would go wild. I thought, *why risk a chance of falling at fifty-something years old*, but he loved the applause. He had solid iron conga drum stands built that could hold his weight. He was a man of about four feet, ten inches tall, so I imagine he weighed around 125 pounds. Tito Puente would joke around, saying Patato shopped in the kids' section for his suits. And well, it was true because I went shopping with him. Someone usually had to accompany him because no one could understand his mumbled speech when he tried to speak in English or Spanish. So, basically, he needed an interpreter—even in Puerto Rico, when he would occasionally go home to visit his wife. It was no wonder his wife didn't mind him not coming home for very long periods of time.

To save some money for shopping in Paris, I found a flight to Belgium and then planned to take the train to Paris. Talk about an exciting trip—it an unforgettable adventure.

Since it was the Christmas vacation from school for my sons, Billy and Miles, we sent them to Indiana to spend the holiday with my sister Sylvia and her family. Her children, Lee and Daniel, were around the same age. I felt that since they had their cousins to play with, they would have a good time and be safe and well-fed by their Aunt Sylvia, who enjoyed cooking large pots of delicious food.

Once I had everything in order, I was ready to travel. I left from Kennedy Airport a day after Jorge and the band, with my arrival being Brussels, Belgium. During the flight, all I thought about was walking along le boulevard Champs-Élysées wearing my fur coat and stopping in one of the shops to buy my favorite perfume, Cabochard de Grès. Then on to sit at a sidewalk café, to have a buttery, flaky croissant, very daintily catching all the crumbs onto the small dish alongside a steaming café au lait in one of those wide coffee bowls that I've only seen in the movies.

I bought a first-class train ticket on the Trans Europ Express to Paris, which was the only option available. I thought, *Wonderful! I'm getting the actual European train experience.* As soon as I slid the wooden door open, I felt like I had stepped into a noir French film. The cabin had a slight musty odor, and as I sat down, I noticed the well-worn, deep red velvet cushion seats of the hundreds, maybe thousands, of travelers before me. I slowly ran my fingers across the velvet, drifting onto the warm softness of the mink, and it lured me into a trance. I felt like an actress traveling across the border into France when the ticket master came around asking for my ticket and passport. I felt elegant and lifted my chin as the attendant returned my passport and said, *'Merci, Madame, Bienvenue en France.'* I answered back with the only word I knew, *Merci,* as I tipped my head and gave a small smile. As he left, I turned to look out of the window and thought, *how exciting.*

The train rolled through short tunnels and passed under small bridges made of wood or of old blackened metal. Worn, dark brick walls made me think of black and white World War II movies, with scenes of soldiers searching the train cars for a villain dressed in a black velvet hat, dark suit, and a cape draped over his shoulders. I felt like a Latina woman traveling in a strange country in search of her missing husband as I ate a delicious Belgian chocolate bar I was given on the plane. I was getting hungry, and between my daydreaming, I also thought about how I would ask for directions to the hotel.

After a couple of hours, the train pulled into the station. Fortunately, I had a small suitcase that I could handle easily, and before I realized it, I was out of the Gare du Nord train station and on the street with people rushing around me, going in all directions. My intention was to hail a cab, but the traffic was moving too fast, and the taxis were not yellow like in Manhattan. I didn't know how I was going to find one since I didn't know what to look for. It certainly was not like New York City back in the day, where we could raise our hand and cabs would pull out of nowhere, trying to get the fare, sometimes almost running you down in the process.

I thought *I must ask someone how I could hail a taxi.* I looked around as people quickly passed me until I spotted a nicely dressed gentleman standing by a telephone booth. I steered towards him because he looked like he might be Spanish, in which case I could ask him for information.

I stepped up and said, "Disculpa, ¿ habla Español?"

I was lucky to have picked him. It turned out he was French but did speak a little Spanish. So, I asked him, "¿dónde puedo conseguir un taxi?"

He explained that I had to go to a taxi stand, pointing across the street. But he said I wouldn't be able to find a cab because it was the rush hour. He suggested it would be easier to take *le métro*. Realizing I didn't speak French, he looked around and spotted two young teen boys. He asked me for the street name, and I said, "Rue de la pe." He explained to the boys to lead me to the subway and direct me to the train I needed to take. They were two students heading home, and they agreed to guide me all the way to *le metro* line that I needed to take.

As they led the way, I followed behind them in my fur coat, rolling my small, grey suitcase. The heels of my Argentine leather boots pounded the walkway, echoing in the pathway. They looked back now and then. When we reached a fork in the underground path, they pointed in the direction I should continue and held up four fingers, indicating four stops. I nodded, managing my "merci" and added "beaucoup." They smiled and waved as they said something in French and continued their journey, chatting away.

I reached the tunnel where my train was pulling up. I quickly pulled my suitcase up and got on. Counting the stops, the train arrived at my destination, and I quickly got off, making my way to climb the stairs out to the street, still comfortable in my boots.

Once outside, I looked around to ask for directions. I spotted a grown-up version of the students, standing in a doorway and looking like they had nowhere to go. There were two males: one Black, and the other with brown skin and black wavy hair. I hoped that maybe one of them spoke Spanish. Again, I made a good choice. It turned out the Latino-looking guy was French but married to a Latina from Colombia. Perfect for me because I could ask where I could find my street, "Rue de la Pe."

They looked at each other and said something in French. I continued to share that I was visiting from NYC and that I would be meeting my husband at the nightclub where he would be rehearsing with the band. The information cleared up the confusion. They chuckled and said that I was mispronouncing the name of the street, as they knew the Salsa club that was on Rue de Lappe. I learned that Lappe has only one syllable, as in "lap," and that, in many cases, the "e" is silent in French words.

With his broken Spanish, I managed to understand that I needed to take the subway to get to Rue de Lappe. They talked among themselves, and I gathered that I would have to return on the subway because it was on the other side of the Seine River, and that they could take me.

I thought about this for a minute and thought since I had already experienced *le métro,* I could do the same by following behind them, feeling safe and free to run if I had to. We agreed that if they took me, I would get them on the guest list to see the show. So once again, I followed my guides and off we went to *le métro.*

As we walked to the train stop, one of them offered to pull my luggage, but I shook my head no and continued marching right behind them. As I made my way down to the station and along the path to catch the train, I felt a bit nervous. Even though they weren't, I tried to think of them as musicians helping me out. After all, they were going to have free passes to get into the popular club of the moment, and I was sure his Colombian wife would thoroughly enjoy dancing to some Latin rhythms. I was of some value to them, getting me there safely, with a fur coat, leather boots, and the grey luggage I was rolling behind me.

We finally arrived at our stop and walked up out of *le métro.* The club was only a block away. Just as we arrived, so did Jorge and the band members. Happy smiles and introductions were made, and the young men received a promise that their names would be on the guest list for Saturday night. They left feeling pretty content.

By this time, all I could think of was the need for a bathroom and then getting something to eat. My stomach was beginning to make peristaltic sounds, which I could hear, having only eaten a small chocolate bar since leaving Belgium. Jorge gave me some francs so I could find some food while they rehearsed.

I walked down the street to a boulangerie, a bakery that sold breads of all different shapes and sizes. In a display case, I spotted a stuffed mini baguette that looked as if it were made for me. It had everything I liked.

Fresh, delicious, and very special, it was stuffed with Jambon de Pays, a savory dry-cured country ham, accompanied by a slice of tomato and a slice of soft Brie cheese. I ordered a café au lait and sat at a small wrought iron table and chair in the front corner of the eating area, where I bit into my sandwich. The tasty mayo mixed with the juicy slice of tomato and the slightly salty taste of the Parma ham, which took my tummy to a happy place. It wasn't quite the picture of the dream I had on the plane, but it didn't fall short in flavor. That's the beauty of living in Europe: having access to local goods and cooking techniques that involve slow fermentation and no preservatives in their doughs for making their breads.

Before leaving the bakery, I ordered three more to take with me. By the time the rehearsal was over, I was exhausted and appreciated going straight to the hotel to share the other sandwiches with Jorge in the hotel room, calling it a night.

The next morning, I was awakened by the sound of the garbage truck making its rounds, and the rays of the sunlight were hitting me in the face through the slit between the curtains. I thought, *Yes, I'm in oh, là là, Paris.* I was glad I wasn't the singer for this gig, so I could be free to roam Paris without having to worry about wearing myself out walking around, reviewing lyrics, attending rehearsals or soundchecks, and stressing about my appearance for the stage. Jorge had some interviews and tasks to attend to regarding the instruments and other matters, so I was on my own.

The first place I wanted to visit was the Louvre to see the Mona Lisa. Months before we even arrived in Paris, Jorge had said to me, "You know, if you shave your eyebrows, you'd look just like her."

I looked at him and said, "You must be crazy if you think I'm going to shave off my eyebrows."

He nudged me, saying, "Yeah, you should shave them off."

I remembered my mother's words: "Careful, girl. Men can say some crazy things, so always follow your own intuition when making decisions, or call me and we'll talk about it."

She didn't actually say that, but I wish she had. I didn't have many close friends, but I was glad I had a mother, and I had my older sister whom I could ask for advice about men.

When I arrived at the museum, there was a line to purchase an entry ticket. I walked around and found my way to the Mona Lisa. There was a small crowd, so I stood in the back as people stared at the painting, making comments as they stepped away, leaving room for me to step closer. As I waited, my first impression was, *goodness, I thought it was bigger.* Seeing it on television or in a magazine, you can't really get a sense of the size unless you know the measurements. Painted by Leonardo da Vinci in 1503, it's only thirty inches by twenty-one inches. As I stepped closer, I kept looking for her eyebrows. They weren't there. I wondered, *did she shave them off?* Maybe she didn't have much facial hair, or perhaps it was a statement by da Vinci—to create a painting that would make people gaze longer at his work. It's a piece of art that sparks questions, but it's impossible to ask an artist who lived five hundred years ago.

Still perusing the painting, I could hear my stomach growling. I thought about the Jambon de Pays and considered eating that delicious sandwich again. I went back to the hotel and caught Jorge and Ray in the lobby, as they were leaving for lunch. I was glad I got back in time to catch them. Jorge was more familiar with Paris from previous trips with George Benson.

We walked and sat at a sidewalk café. We managed to order three café au laits. I also wanted a glass of water, but it was challenging to say *un verre d'eau.* After several rounds of miming, the server finally brought the glass of water with an attitude because I couldn't nail the nasal sound. Still, we pointed from the menu to the steak au poivre—what some call the "poor man's steak." It's a thin steak in a rich gravy made with a bit of heavy cream, brandy, butter, whole peppercorns, and finely chopped parsley. Nothing poor about it. It's delicious, especially with a piece of *pain poilâne*, a French wholewheat bread; a perfect pairing.

I would have practiced some French words, but I didn't have the time to start learning something that could probably take me six months to master, especially the nasal sounds. However, we managed to learn a few words along the way. Now that I do speak some French, I realize I could have learned it, as many words are very similar to those in Spanish and Portuguese. After all, they're all Romance languages.

We left and started following Jorge as he led us to the grand, wide, eight-lane *boulevard Champs-Elysées*, which was lined with horse chestnut trees that bloom with white flowers. Unfortunately, it was winter, but I vowed to return one day in late spring to see the shower of petals from the flowering trees. We strolled, admiring the storefront windows, and picked up beautiful perfume scents as we passed the French ladies strolling and shopping. I felt like I fit right in with my mink coat, but I felt a bit intimidated because I didn't know the language. *Perhaps*, I thought, *I should just buy it at Saks Fifth Avenue in New York and instead use the money to buy something I can't find back home.*

We continued walking and eventually arrived at the Arc de Triomphe, an arch commissioned by Napoleon Bonaparte in 1806 to honor those who fought in battles defending France, symbolizing their patriotism. Decorated along the sides of the great structure are scenes of battles and celebrations of French victories. On the inner walls are engraved the names of generals and battles. An eternal flame burns to honor the fallen, sitting at the head of the tomb and rekindled each evening. We gave our salute and admired the soldiers standing at attention. Since we were the only tourists at the moment, we unapologetically took our time taking pictures before heading back to the hotel.

As I carefully stepped on the cobblestone streets near the hotel, I noticed inlaid laurel crown patterns decorating the façades of buildings, and black wrought-iron gates topped with the Fleur de Lis on each iron rod of the imposing iron doors. Looking up the sides of some buildings, I saw wrought iron balconies with intricate designs. Giant flowerpots and urns adorned the entrances of old stately homes of the aristocrats, museums, government buildings, and parks. The Fleur de Lis was present on doors and door knockers, and probably more places if I had kept searching. However, I gave up, not knowing the full history, but I could confirm with my own eyes the unmistakable French influence in Argentina.

We arrived at the hotel just in time for me to take a nap while the band headed to the club to set up for the evening's gig.

I woke up to the sound of Jorge jangling the keys to the room. "Get up, we don't have much time if you want to go to the club tonight."

I quickly jumped into the shower after Jorge and got dressed as fast as I could. We were out of the hotel and on our way to the club. As soon as we arrived, I spotted Allan and Michel with their wives. After a bit of a hustle with the doorman, we all made our way inside. The place was already packed, and the DJ was playing salsa music by Eddie Palmieri from the *Live at Sing Sing* album. People were dancing, laughing, and drinking. I pointed to a table reserved for the band, where my guests and I sat, trying to talk, but it was impossible over the loud music.

Everyone seemed to be having a great time already. Slowly, the DJ lowered the music as the band started the intro of the first song, and the spotlights on the stage grew brighter. People started applauding, eagerly waiting for the show to begin. Song after song, the crowd either danced or stood in front of the stage, watching each musician do their thing. Jorge rolled out the melodies up and down the keyboard, the percussion hitting strong. Artie Webb, the flute player, jumped on two feet as he blew through his flute, hitting high notes that even surprised him. Then it was Patato's turn. He took his signature two-tone Kangol cap, snatched it off his head, and hit the conga drum a few times. The crowd went wild. Then, he climbed up onto the congas. As Jorge played the introduction of *On Broadway*, Patato started tapping to the beat. Once again, the audience went wild as he jumped down. I kept thinking, *oh my Lord, I hope he lands safely*. He landed like a cool, slick cat. He looked up at everyone, did a little arm breakdance move, and snuck back in behind his drums.

The show finally came to an end. My new French friends gave me hugs and kisses, thanking me as they said goodbye with smiles from ear to ear.

It was now 2:00 a.m. and we were hungry, so Jorge took Sergio Brandão, the bass player, and me to a restaurant he knew would be open. We walked along the cobblestone streets, which were empty, quiet, and mysterious, as it was our first time on these dark, narrow paths. Sergio and I exchanged questioning glances as we followed Jorge.

We arrived at the Notre Dame Cathedral, and it was truly awe-inspiring. As we walked around the front, we looked up at the many kings of Judah, their marble eyes that seemed to follow us. We marveled at the intricate details of so many statues, which perfectly complemented the Gothic architecture, including the soaring flying buttresses. The scene exuded an eerie atmosphere in the dark, cool winter breeze. Standing under so many statues, I felt an unsettling sensation that the eyes were watching me intensely as I walked to the left and right of the façade.

We continued to walk behind Jorge, down the street and through an alley, exchanging glances as Sergio and I wondered, *Where is he taking us?* Finally, we reached a big, heavy wooden door. Jorge slowly opened it, and to our surprise, we stepped into a dimly lit space with rustic brick walls, a bar, and people sitting at small round tables, quietly talking in French while sipping wine and having foie gras (goose liver pâté) with mango chutney, Sauternes wine jelly, and fig jam—the specialty of the house. We both raised our eyebrows, and I thought, *ooh là la, this looks delicious*!

The next few days were just as exciting, with the house packed as the weekend approached. I got to sing a couple of times, so I had my thrill. On the final night, the house was packed again. Word had spread around town, so when we arrived at the club, there was a line down the block of people without tickets wanting to get in. I sat at the table with some Argentinian friends of Jorge's, but the noise around us drowned out the conversation, so I decided to accept a dance from a very handsome guy I'd been watching as he danced with various ladies. I ended up dancing with him the rest of the night. Remember, I was a dance teacher, so I had no problem keeping up, and he had a great time leading me through turns. I had a wonderful time as well.

As the final night came to an end, we all had to leave in the morning. I had to catch the train back to Belgium to make my flight, while Jorge and the band had a later flight. So, we all helped pack up the instruments—even Jorge's friend and his wife. He kept talking the whole time, asking Jorge for changes to a song and suggesting that he come to the hotel so Jorge could write out the music. Jorge had a late flight the next day, so he figured he had time to visit with his friend, since it was impossible to have a real conversation in the crowded club.

Walking back to the hotel, amid the chatter of voices, I told Jorge that I had to arrive at the Gare du Nord train station by 7:30 a.m. He said, "Okay," and continued his conversation with his friend.

We were in the room, and the guy kept talking even as Jorge was writing out the piece of music. I kept glancing at the clock as I finished packing my suitcase, now just watching the time tick away. I nudged Jorge a couple of times, but the conversation kept going, with laughter and wine glasses being refilled. It was 7:10 a.m. when I finally said, "I have to leave now."

As I grabbed my coat, I started leading everyone out of the room. The guy kept talking all the way to the street. I shouted, "GOODBYE!" and Jorge followed behind me.

He asked what time I had to be at the train. When I told him 7:30 a.m., he shouted, "No way! Why didn't you say anything?"

I looked at him and yelled, "I DID! MANY TIMES!"

When we arrived at the station, I knew exactly where I had to go. We ran toward the platform, but we were too late. I saw my train pulling away. I screamed, "NO!" Jorge shouted profanities in Spanish. He was carrying my suitcase, and in a moment of frustration, he threw it to the ground and started kicking it. "You'd bettershow up in New York City safely with my money from the gig," he yelled.

It was several thousand francs he didn't want to carry through customs, hoping to avoid paying tax. I had the money tucked safely in a cloth sack inside an inner pocket of my fur coat. I was very thin back then, so no one would suspect that anything was hidden under my coat. In 1981, it was still relatively easy to pass through customs—unless customs officials had strong suspicions that something was amiss.

He finally stopped kicking my suitcase with those leather boots of his and said, "Call someone and see where you can stay in Paris and take the train in the morning."

I looked at him and said, "Just leave. I'll see you at home."

He stormed off. I stood there, wondering what to do next. I loved that man too much to do anything silly. I called one of Patato's friends who came to the club every night, but when I reached her, she said she was leaving in a couple of hours to visit her mother in the countryside. I decided then that

I would just take the next train and get to the airport. Maybe there would be another flight I could catch.

On the train to the airport, the image of Jorge kicking my suitcase and swearing in Spanish felt like a scene straight out of a movie. Now, I felt like Sophia Loren, draped in my fur, the weight of thousands of francs tucked inside my coat, small bills from the money collected at the door and behind the bar from drinks sold. I thought, *what if I get stopped at customs? What would I say? What would Sophia Loren do?* I smiled to myself, imagining her cool, calm demeanor. She would probably smile and ask, "How much is the tax, officer?"

Yes, that's what I would do. There was no reason to get all worked up, kicking my suitcase, and shouting at me. I suppose that was just stress being released from the week-long gig, dealing with the details and the musicians. We loved each other very much, but sometimes the stress just took over and had to come out in some way. Fortunately, I was able to remain calm and handle the screaming. I should have left the hotel earlier, and I'm sure they would have followed me out.

I arrived at the airport and went straight to the counter. My Belgium airline ticket agent told me I couldn't use my ticket with another airline and that the next flight was fully booked. Unless someone didn't show up or missed their flight, I would have to wait until the following day. Now, I was stuck at the airport, waiting to see if anyone would miss the flight.

What would Sophia Loren do in this case? I thought. She'd probably call someone to pick her up at the airport—she'd have many friends in Paris who would love to do that. Ha! But not me. This was my first time in Europe. So, with no one to call, I considered staying in a hotel, as I had the money to do so. But then, I realized I'd be alone—a young, good-looking gal in a fur coat lined with francs. I thought for a moment, then decided, *Not a good idea.* I figured I was probably better off staying in the airport.

Walking around the airport, I looked up at the flight information board. Rome, Italy, leaving at 8:00 p.m., Athens, Greece, leaving at 8:15 p.m. For about sixty seconds, I thought about buying a ticket to Greece and cursing Jorge and his attitude, kicking my luggage. I could have a great time with all those francs. But that fantasy didn't last very long as my feet began to signal to me that it was time to give them a break. I stopped in a restaurant to eat before heading back to the ticket counter, hoping for some sign from the clerk. But that sign never came. One last time, I approached her, and she said, "No, sorry. Everyone has checked in."

I walked away, thinking, *Damn, now what?*

Now what? I guessed I would just stay there in the airport. There had to be a safe place to sit and fall asleep. I managed to doze off but woke up around 11:00 p.m. and started walking around the empty airport, with only a few cleaning staff and ticket agents in sight. I passed a couple of young guys sleeping on the floor between the rows of seats. I was exhausted because I hadn't slept all night, and here it was, night again. I wondered if there was another spot where I could fall asleep and feel safe.

I walked down to the first floor and wandered into a hall with several rooms. I entered through an open wooden door and found an empty chapel. The small space was lit by the dancing faux flames of tea candles set in red glass holders, casting their warm glow onto the walls. Framed pictures of angels adorned the space, and eight rows of benches faced a golden cross. I thought this would be my safe place to hang out until morning. Surely no one would come in, and if I closed the doors, anyone passing by would assume they were locked. I closed the doors and sat down to finally remove my boots. I said a few prayers and eventually drifted off to sleep on one of the benches.

When I opened my eyes, I quickly sat up and saw it was 6:00 a.m. Feeling thankful, I left the chapel feeling rested. My coat provided a good layer of comfort while I slept on the wooden bench. I went back upstairs to the ticket counter, and surprisingly, the clerk said I could take the very next flight, leaving in an hour. I was overjoyed to hear that. I thanked my guardian angel for watching over me and for making sure I didn't oversleep.

As I sat on the plane returning home, I thought about how I would simply take a cab and walk through the door like nothing had happened, like I'd had a wonderful time sleeping in the airport. I also hoped that Jorge hadn't broken my white French teapot or the porcelain fromagerie plates I'd packed in his suitcase. They were the only souvenirs I'd bought. Still, despite everything, I couldn't help but smile. What a birthday adventure I was bringing home with me.

When it's time to go, don't just say it—move. Say GOODBYE!
Walk to the door and let your steps speak for you.

CHAPTER FIVE

Mario Bauza's Mambo Kings

t was a sunny Sunday morning in June, and I lay dawdling in my bed under a cozy blanket listening to a group of riders as they passed under my eighth-floor window on their way to the horse trail in Central Park. I always enjoyed the sound of each hoof as it hit the pavement in a steady, rhythmic, and gentle beat, finding it so soothing as the sound echoed between the brick high-rise across the street and my building.

I lay there, thinking that I should sign up for lessons soon—before they sell the old garage building that served as their barn, or I would miss the opportunity for riding lessons.

Sunday mornings were usually a leisurely day. The boys would sleep in, and I would stay in bed until they got up because they would want their pancakes and crispy bacon for a late breakfast. Sometimes, it was hard to get out of bed as I held on to my dreams of being with Jorge and the boys, having fun, going on vacations, and watching them grow.

It had been a few years since Jorge died of cancer, and since then, I had to focus more on how to run the household financially. To land better-paying gigs, I knew I needed to record my first music CD. After fifteen years of marriage, I now had to be the breadwinner. It was time to secure more concerts, jazz club gigs, and workshops, leaving the restaurants and weddings behind.

The wedding gigs always depressed me. Standing on stage, singing soft ballads while the bride and groom shared their first dance, followed by the routine of the wedding party joining in—it all brought back memories of romance and love. The part I hated most, though, was the cutting of the cake. I had seen it too many times: the bride, with her beautifully decorated cake, having it smeared across her face, ruining her expensive makeup. Then, she'd run off to lock herself in the bathroom, embarrassed, with her mother chasing after her and the new in-laws standing at the edge of the dance floor, unsure of what to do.

But between the chaos of the evening and the band blaring distracting music, I couldn't help but fantasize about remarrying—wearing a white dress with a long lace train, having a three-tiered cake, and receiving a diamond ring—things I never had in my first marriage. Of course, that marriage was filled with excitement, beautiful memories, and two wonderful sons. We carried each other through tough times with plenty of love.

The ringing of the red desk phone startled me out of my daydream. It was my friend, Dr. Manuel Sanchez Acosta.

"Oye, Adela." I could hear the excitement in his authoritative voice. "Go to Mario Bauza's house first thing tomorrow morning and tell him you can cover for Graciela on the tour to Europe."

He explained that he'd suggested Graciela not go with the band, because the tour would be too much stress on her knees. She carried some extra weight, which didn't help, and her blood pressure was a little elevated. The three-week tour would involve flying to Europe, then traveling by plane and bus to perform at jazz festivals across several countries.

I was still in a fog from sleep when I hung up the phone. Was this a dream? Could this really be happening? I was getting my chance to sing with the top Afro-Cuban jazz orchestra. Could I finally step into Graciela's shoes?

The adrenaline started rushing through me. I jumped out of bed, quickly got dressed, and retreated to my safe place: the kitchen. As I pulled ingredients out of the fridge, I kept wondering—would Mario hire me? I knew I was capable of doing the job. Yes, I, a Mexican American, a Chicana, singing to Cuban mambo rhythms. But what would Graciela say? Would she give me her blessing?

I whipped the pancake batter as my thoughts raced. Finally, the pancakes were flipped, and the maple-flavored bacon began to sizzle. The delicious aroma quickly brought the boys to the table. As we ate, I told them about the phone call from Dr. Acosta, the family doctor for many of us musicians in the Mario Bauza circle of friends.

Mario Bauza was a Cuban musician who arrived in New York City in the early '30s and landed a seat playing trumpet with the Chick Webb orchestra. It was there he met Dizzy Gillespie. So impressed with Dizzy's talent, Mario decided to give him the opportunity to take his place, as his brother-in-law, Frank "Machito" Grillo, had just arrived from Cuba and planned to start their own musical group—the Afro-Cubans. When Machito entered military service in 1941, he sent for his sister, Graciela, to come from Cuba to take his place until he returned.

Graciela Pérez was already a young professional singer in Cuba, having sung with various music groups, including one of the first all-female orchestras, Anacaona, alongside her sister Estella, who was married to Mario Bauza. Once Machito returned from service, he and Graciela became the lead singers of the renamed Machito Orchestra, led by Mario Bauza. The orchestra played at the famed Savoy and Palladium Ballrooms, which opened in the

1940s to cater to mambo and swing dancers, and later incorporated salsa music that was gaining popularity by the early 1970s.

Mambo, a Cuban genre, and salsa, created in Manhattan by Puerto Rican musicians like timbal player Tito Puente, a Juilliard graduate, became the heart of the scene. Puerto Rican singer Tito Rodríguez also made waves, driving ladies to line up outside clubs hoping to hear their heartthrob perform. Often, the three bands—Machito's, Tito Puente's, and the singer Tito Rodrigues—shared the stage, creating thrilling 'battle of the bands' performances that had the mixed audience of Puerto Ricans, African Americans, and Jewish dancers wild with excitement over the fiery rhythms.

After years of performing stateside, in 1981, Machito was offered the chance to perform in Europe for the first time, but with a smaller ensemble due to the high costs of travel. This led to a disagreement about the band's future. The smaller group required Mario Bauza and Graciela to stay in New York, as they had existing engagements with the Machito Orchestra. After Machito returned from the successful short tour, Mario, who had always opposed breaking up the band, decided to form a new group with Graciela. This decision eventually led to The Mario Bauza Afro-Cuban Jazz Orchestra—an ensemble that recorded three CDs and continued performing until Mario died in 1993.

Graciela, meanwhile, continued to perform in a few tributes, keeping her presence alive in the music world until her passing in 2010. After Machito died in 1984, his son, Mario Grillo, took up the baton of the family orchestra—though, in his case, the baton was really the drumsticks of his timbales. He carried on the family legacy of seventy-five years until his death in September 2024.

Now it was 1992, and the thought of standing in for Graciela was a huge deal for me. It wasn't just about the gig—it was about stepping into her shoes, filling a space that had always been hers. I wanted to prove to myself and to the band that I could do it, but I also needed to make sure Billy and Miles would be okay while I was gone.

I asked them if they could manage for three weeks, with the wooden money box refilled for food and emergencies, and my brother staying to look out for them. The most they could do would be to invite their friends over to work on music and order pizzas. Billy was already working at Carmine's, bringing home great leftovers from the takeout kitchen, so I didn't have to worry about them feeding themselves. After all, we lived in a neighborhood where you could find all kinds of food on Columbus and Amsterdam Avenues. I also made sure they had the newest computer and programs, so they'd be more inclined to stay home, immersed in their music, rather than getting distracted by going out where trouble might find them.

The gig was in July, so the boys would be on summer vacation from school. But still, it felt like a big leap—one that both excited and terrified me.

Billy had been hoping for a good gig to come through because he had plans to buy a used car for the fall semester at the Bronx High School of Science. It was one of the top three schools in the city, despite our location on the west side of Manhattan. Miles didn't have much to say about it—he was mostly absorbed in his music programs, learning how to make beats on the computer.

After their father passed, Billy stepped up to take charge, watching over Miles, even though they were only a year apart. I trusted Billy to do the right thing while I was gone. Before the Spike Lee movie came out, I'd always say, "Now please, do the right thing," before closing the door behind me and heading out to work.

But here I was today, my mind racing. Would Mario say yes? It was too bad I had to wait until morning to see him. Dr. Acosta had mentioned that Mario would be at an event all day. I wondered if his wife knew what was going on. I called her to ask, and she was happy to receive my call. She said several young singers had been hanging around Graciela's apartment in the past few days, trying to step in, but they weren't professional singers. She felt I should be the one to go.

I was relieved to hear this because I knew I was the only singer around who could fit in perfectly to do the job. But offstage, I was somewhat timid—not aggressive enough to ask for things unless directed. I thought, *Thank God I had Dr. Acosta on my side.* He must have visited Graciela and heard what was happening to give me the heads-up. Not only was he a doctor, but also a Dominican music composer who played piano on several songs that had been repeatedly recorded. His recommendation for me to take Graciela's place came from a musician's professional point of view.

It only made sense to have someone with a powerful voice, like Graciela's, to stand in front of the sixteen-piece orchestra, especially with its strong Latin percussion section—musicians like Carlos "Patato" Valdez and Joe Gonzalez, who could drive the cowbell to lift the orchestra to new musical heights, and Bobby Sanabria, whose South Bronx fire was always evident in his drumming. I'd already performed with them in other bands, so they were no strangers to me.

When it came to song selection, I pulled out my Ray Santos arrangement of Jorge's original *Reflexionando* (Reflecting) and began deciding which of Graciela's charts I should sing. Although I was familiar with her repertoire, I spent the rest of the day learning *"Deja Que Hablen" (Let Them Talk), a powerful mambo that was* one of my favorites from her recordings. Fortunately, it was in my vocal range—or, as we musicians say, it was in my key. With this historic orchestra and these great songs, I felt ready to step in for the legendary Graciela Pérez.

The warm, brilliant sun slowly crept in between the split of my bedroom curtains, but it was the alarm that woke me. I quickly jumped out of bed and got ready to see Mario. He lived several blocks up from me on Columbus Avenue. I took the bus up Amsterdam Avenue and got off at 108th street to walk over one block to Columbus Ave. It was a quick ride since I lived on 89th and Columbus Ave.

I rang the bell, but there was no answer. I knew Lourdes, his wife, would be at work, but I was expecting Mario to be home since he was an early riser. I rang a few more times, but still no answer.

There was a phone booth on the corner—remember those? I called his apartment, but the answering machine picked up. I then called Dr. Acosta, and he suggested I go to the cleaners around the corner, where Mario would sometimes hang out with the owner and other friends who'd drop in.

When I walked into the cleaners, I didn't recognize anyone, but they knew me as Jorge's widow and a singer. Right away, they assumed I was looking for Mario and told me he had a doctor's appointment but would eventually head back to his apartment. I thanked them and returned to the phone booth.

I called my comadre Dina Ramos, my son Miles's godmother, to share the news. She was thrilled for me and encouraged me to stay put and wait for Mario to show up. She asked what I was going to wear, and I said, "Wait, I don't know if I have the gig yet! I'll let you know when I know. Right now, I'm hungry and need a bathroom. I'll call you later. Bye!"

"Bye!"

After returning with a sandwich, I was swallowing the last bite when I saw Mario coming around the corner. He spotted me, came right over, and said, "What'cha doing here?"

"Waiting for you," I replied.

I explained that Dr. Acosta had called to say Graciela wasn't going on the tour and that he "told me to come see you, to let you know that her songs are in my key and that I could do the job."

Mario gave me a concerned look, his jaw slightly dropped, his bottom lip hanging, and his eyes were almost hidden behind his murky lenses as he processed the information. But he quickly recovered and said, "Okay! Call Michel, the manager, and tomorrow morning, meet me here at 8:00 a.m. to go to the passport office!"

I had a passport, but apparently, Patato and Diorius Rivera, one of the saxophone players, didn't have one. Patato was Cuban, and Diorius came as a child from the Dominican Republic and never traveled out of the US.

"Yes, yes," I said excitedly.

I hugged him and rushed back to the phone booth to call Michel, the manager, telling him I was on the gig and that I'd give him my passport information once I got home. I also told him I would be going to the Cuban Embassy with Mario to try to get a passport for Patato.

As soon as I opened the door to my empty apartment, I shouted, "Woo hoo!"

Then I got to work, pulling out my passport and making calls. The boys arrived from school just as Dina answered her phone. I couldn't wait to tell her, so I shouted, "I got the gig!"

The boys heard the news, and Billy was thrilled—he had already started searching the ads for a used car. The gig was a three-week tour, beginning in London, where we would connect to Verona, Italy, for the first concert. From there, we would travel by tour bus or plane to perform at various jazz festivals, including the Montreux Jazz Festival in Switzerland, the Pori Jazz Festival in Finland, and Tivoli Gardens in Denmark, as well as in other countries such as Norway, Germany, Italy, and France, and the North Sea Festival in the Netherlands.

The next couple of weeks were a whirlwind of preparations for the trip. I spent hours preparing my outfits and practicing the songs on my own, so that when it was my turn at rehearsal, it only took twenty minutes. I was ready. The show would run for an hour and a half. I'd sing two songs, the male singer in the band, Rudy Calzado, would sing two, and the band would play the rest. The rehearsal already had the fiery energy of the great musicians who knew how to put on a show. Even Carlos "Patato" Valdez would be there, with no passport but with a special permission signed for him to travel out of the United States. But he wouldn't be tap-dancing on his congas anymore. Age was catching up with him, and his body was no longer up for it, but he knew how to get his extra cheers by grabbing his Kangol cap and slapping his conga.

The day to depart finally came. I hugged my boys and told my brother Jesse, "Please, do the right thing."

They reassured me not to worry and to take care of myself. I wasn't worried about being on the road with so many men. There were two other women—Lilly White, who played the saxophone and was my roommate in some cities, and Tatiana, the daughter of Mr. Calzado, who went as an assistant. The guys in the band were like big brothers who would watch my back, having known me since I first arrived in New York at nineteen with Jorge, and now, as a widowed mother raising two boys. I was always treated with respect.

The day before we left, I'd been secretly hired by the booking agent to stay by Mario Bauzá's side due to his advanced age. At eighty-one, I had to make sure he took his blood pressure pill. Mario always carried his leather music bag, packed with approximately twenty music charts for the band's sixteen members. That meant many sheets of music paper, plus the weight of the leather case itself. Can you imagine how heavy that must've been? The only person he'd let carry that bag was Victor Paz, the Panamanian first trumpet player who had played on countless Broadway shows. Victor was over six feet tall and strong enough to handle the weight of the music bag, as we made our way through many countries.

At the airport, I offered Mario the chance to put the leather bag on my rolling luggage cart (remember those?), since my baggage had already been checked in, but he refused several times. It wasn't until we were in an airport somewhere in Germany that he looked at me in despair. He was short of breath, so I sat him down to let him take his pill and drink some water. That's when I said, "Give me that bag!"

I placed it on my luggage rack and secured a strap tightly around it.

He looked at me and said, "Okay, but I'm going to roll it."

I replied, "No, you're not. My music is in that case too, and I'm not going to lose my music. Besides, you should let me roll you around in an airport wheelchair. Look over there."

It was Cab Calloway in a wheelchair, looking happy because his musicians were rolling him around to conserve his energy for his performances.

Mario said, "No-no-no-no, but you can roll the music. Just stay close to me."

I finally took that load off his hands, and he didn't have any more incidents for the rest of the trip. But every time we crossed paths with Cab Calloway, I would say, "See, now that's the way to get around in an airport."

THE VERONA JAZZ FESTIVAL

After arriving in London, we caught a connecting flight to Verona, Italy. Upon landing, all twenty-one of us piled onto a tour bus—sixteen musicians, two singers, Mario, the band leader, one assistant, and Maurice Cohen, the tour manager. The drive was stunning. We wound our way along roads lined with tall cypress trees, some so narrow that only one car could pass at a time. Old and modern houses sat side by side, propping each other up in the medieval section of town. We were headed to the Teatro Romano, eager to arrive in time for the sound check.

We were just about there when our bus driver made a questionable decision. He must've looked down the street and thought the modern luxury bus could fit through. But as we started down the narrow path, about a third of the way in, the musicians began peering out the windows; some even stood and leaned over the seats to see how tight the space really was. Voices grew louder and rowdier as they argued in both English and Spanish whether the bus would make it through.

Someone joked, "I bet you a cold beer it can't get through!"

He was one of those who sounded like he'd rather be anywhere else, and honestly, I didn't want to be stuck in a bus either.

At that point, Mario stood up and said, "Everybody sit down and shut up. The man knows what he's doing."

But of course, there's always one in the group who has to keep going. "The bus *will* get stuck. We won't be able to open the door to get out, nah, he's got to go back!"

Sure enough, the driver decided to back up. It was one of those moments when you realized we were deep in an area designed for carts and horses, not buses. The streets in the older part of Verona were so narrow that they could fit only one European car at a time. Verona, of course, was famous for being the setting of Shakespeare's *Romeo and Juliet*, and I could see how the city's beauty might've inspired him. The narrow streets, the pale pastel buildings made of timber and stone, the wooden shutters with heavy hinges, and the carved iron balconies draped in flowers—everything felt like it came out of a romantic dream. You could almost imagine Juliet looking out over the balcony, waiting for Romeo to call her name.

We managed to arrive at the Teatro Romano and were amazed to find this ancient yet well-preserved Roman venue, built in the first century. It was hard to believe—between AD 1 and 100—and here we were in 1992. I could hardly wrap my mind around the fact that I was standing on the very stage where, perhaps, Shakespeare had once presented his plays. The theater had semi-circular seating that offered a breathtaking view of the Adige River and the city beyond. The seating was made up of weathered stone steps, and as I stood on stage, vocalizing, my voice echoed through the empty space. It felt like I was stepping into a medieval dream.

One of the dresses I brought, with its golden threads and hues of yellow, orange, and touches of green, would be perfect against the backdrop of the seasoned bricks from the original walls.

We were then led below, under the stage, where we were told that the subterranean rooms had once housed lions for events like those we'd seen in movies with gladiators battling for the crowd's thrill. Now, the rooms had been converted into dining areas where we'd be served a meal after the show. Other rooms were used for storing stage equipment. It was surreal, this mix of ancient history—lions, Shakespeare, and now us: Mario and his Mambo Kings. The stage name was a nod to the *Mambo Kings Play Love Songs* movie that had just been released.

After the incredible show, with an audience that clapped enthusiastically, I remember thinking, *So, when do the lions come out? And where's the dressing room for the handsome, muscle-bound gladiators? Also, what's on the menu?* I was hungry again.

After the show, we hung out in the hotel bar, talking about what was next. The next venue would be the Zelt Musik Festival in Freiburg, Germany. We were leaving the very next day to catch a flight, then share a two-hour bus ride to the venue with musicians from the Cab Calloway band.

ZELT MUSIK FESTIVAL IN FREIBURG, GERMANY

The two-and-a-half-hour bus ride from the airport to the festival fairgrounds was mostly quiet. Some musicians were reading or listening to music with their headphones, while others engaged in quiet conversations with their seatmates or napped as we made our way to the beautiful hotel.

Since I was standing in for Graciela, I was fortunate enough to have my own room in several cities, which allowed me to enjoy a bit of the 'star status.' I could lay out my clothes, shoes, and cosmetics without taking up a roommate's space. I could also make my phone calls to check up on the boys without disturbing anyone with my voice, sharing my excitement with them.

The boys reassured me that they were doing fine. Billy told me that he had found a car and that my brother would drive him to check it out. At only fifteen, soon to be sixteen, Billy already had the ambition that was going to take him places and help him accomplish many things. This was just the beginning.

After saying goodbye to my boys, I had some time to take a nap since we didn't have to perform until the following day. I had agreed to go to the fairgrounds with a couple of the musicians to check out some of the performances, since it was our night off.

I slept for a while before waking to the sound of melodious church bells. As I got up to look out the window, I counted three stone-carved steeple towers in close proximity, each taking turns announcing the 6:00 hour. They stood against a backdrop of tall Norway spruces and other pines of the Black Forest.

I learned that half of Freiburg's population is Christian, and they built one of the oldest Gothic churches—the Cathedral of Our Lady (Freiburger Münster)—around 1130, finishing by 1200. The church was built to accommodate the growing town, serving as a place for gatherings, festivals, and masses. It later became the seat for the bishop. Miraculously, the cathedral survived WWII. The irreplaceable stained-glass windows were saved by removing them, storing them in hiding, and rehanging them after the war.

Visiting this cathedral, I realized how much artistic beauty and history are embedded in these places of worship. The architecture, the stone statues, tapestries, paintings, and even the sculptured wood on entrance doors and facades with each element telling a story of the period in which it was created. Many now feature ornate, majestic organs, which complete the immersive experience of attending a Mass.

A few years later, on a tour through several cities in Spain, my roommate and I made it a point to visit the cathedral or main church in every city we could, along with the best wine shop, if time allowed. We had a wonderful, memorable time in Spain, often recalling our tour in Germany.

I headed out to join the fellows waiting for me outside the hotel. As we walked the short distance, I noticed the many people passing us on bicycles. When we arrived at the festival, we saw two very long rows of bikes parked, with no cars in sight. Germany was already well-known for its recycling program, and it was very noticeable. There wasn't any paper or garbage on the ground. We wandered around, stopping at various tents to examine the crafts, which were quite interesting. There were earrings and other wearable art pieces made from recycled rubber tires, recycled jeans transformed into various outfits, and souvenirs crafted from wood and plastic bottle caps.

Stepping into a food tent, I looked for something to satisfy my appetite. I ordered a plate of cheese, dry sausage, cut apples, crackers, and foie gras with apple chutney. It was served on a wafer as the plate—every crumb was edible. The napkin was small made of cloth, so you could reuse it. Drinks were served in returnable glasses and mugs, and we would receive our deposit back on returns. I was impressed by the focus on recycling. Everything at the festival was recyclable, clean, and so well-organized. Back in the United States in 1991, we hadn't even begun to promote recycling yet.

The next day came, and everything moved like clockwork. The bus came to pick us up, along with the musicians of the Cab Calloway Orchestra. While we went to soundcheck, they went to the performers' dining tent, as they would be performing after us. After checking the mics and making sure the stage was set with colored spotlights aimed in the right places, we were ready to hit it by 8:00 p.m.—showtime.

The upbeat crowd was waiting for us, some sitting, some standing in small groups, talking and interspersed with soft laughter. A couple of people stood off to the side of the stage, waiting to greet some of the musicians as they stepped out, holding their instruments and taking their seats behind their music stands. Once everyone was in place and the band was introduced, Mario Bauza counted, quickly "One, two. One, two, three, four."

The sound from the trumpets soared over the heads of the audience, and the percussion, accompanied by the drums, began building a fiery rhythm. The piano and saxes played the melody, while the bass punched the souls of the people. We walloped them with our Latin rhythms. While I was singing, I saw people trying to move their bodies to the beat, attempting to dance. Some just bounced, bending their knees with smiles of delight, possibly experiencing their first live Latin music performance.

We ended our show, and the audience kept cheering, wanting more. They didn't want us to leave the stage, but we could not extend our time because Cab Calloway was standing in the wings, dressed in his spats and white long-tailed tuxedo, ready to put on his show. And what a show it was! I watched from the side of the stage as he performed his most famous hit, "Minnie the Moocher." He danced as he sang and scatted, inviting the audience to follow his vocalese. I even joined in.

He had this gimmick of holding onto one of his high notes for what must have been over a minute. The audience went wild. Before the end of the song, he held that high note again, longer than the one before. Again, the audience cheered wildly. I was amazed at the energy he put out from his eighty-three-year-old body.

Check out a short film called *Cab Calloway's Hi-De-Ho (1934), among his many appearances in movies available on YouTube,* to enjoy his performance. A true performer, Cab was always singing and dancing while conducting the orchestra. He was also a very snappy dresser off the stage, with his Zoot Suits and wide-rimmed, flamboyant hats made of smooth felt, complete with a large, fluffy feather that bounced as he swaggered along.

We continued the tour through the beautiful cities of Lugano, Switzerland, and the Vienne Jazz Festival in France, followed by the Montreux Jazz Festival in Switzerland. These were all remarkable cities, filled with historical culture dating back to medieval times, beautiful people wearing European clothing styles, delicious food made from local produce, and towns situated by romantic, scenic lakes. The festivals and the towns were definitely "wanna go back" kind of places.

Moving on through our itinerary, we were finally heading to our last stop of the tour: Perugia, Italy, by way of Pori, Finland. It was a long distance, and when you've been traveling for many days by airplanes and tour buses—going to sound checks, eating, performing, back to the hotel, then leaving in the morning to travel to the next stop—it starts to take a toll. Some stops were great because we had layover days, where we could sleep without early risers banging on the door, saying, "Get up!"

Alternatively, we could enjoy some sightseeing, visit a cathedral or museum, and pick up some local wine, cheese, and cured ham to enjoy on the bus.

After the show in Pori, we boarded a bus for an hour and a half to get to the hotel for the night. We stopped along the way at a diner, where we had a delay. We finally arrived at a motel around 3:00 a.m. Exhausted, we were told we'd have to leave at 6:00 a.m. to get to the airport for our flight. I never took my clothes off. As soon as my head hit the pillow, I was jolted awake by a banging on the wall behind my headboard. It didn't take me long to figure out what it could be. After all, we had arrived at a motel and were led down a dark hallway on the ground floor. For all I knew, it could've been a three-hour, couples-only hotel. That's what I think, but whatever—it was clean, at least.

We were now on our way to the airport to catch a flight from Turku, Finland, to Stockholm, Sweden, and then another flight from Stockholm to Rome, Italy. We were thrilled to finally be heading to warmer weather, as the trip north had been rainy, damp, and chilly. After eating nothing but cured fish for breakfast, lunch, and dinner, Italian food was definitely on my mind.

The Rome flight arrived late due to a problem with our plane, so we had to wait for a replacement. We finally got on our way, but we were running behind. The plan was to arrive directly at the venue for a sound check, then check into the hotel and eat before returning for an 8:00 p.m. performance.

Our bus ride from the airport to Perugia for our final concert was an incredible journey. As tired as I was, I couldn't stop looking out of the window, taking in the charm of beautiful Italy. Many flowers created a rich tapestry of nature, with tall, thin cypress trees and other greenery among the ancient buildings, mixed with the modern. Wild red poppies were bursting with color, lavender decorating the doorways of old brick homes, and oleander shrubs with their pink, red, and white blossoms lining the narrow, winding road to Perugia.

Driving up and around the hill, I could see the red terracotta tiles, and I never thought a roof could be so beautiful. The road circled the hill until we reached the top, where a town of historic homes and shops lined the medieval buildings, all set along tidy streets.

We finally arrived—late. There wasn't any time to check into the hotel, but the bus did stop to let me off. Mario said, "You get some rest, and someone will be back to pick you up at 7:30 because showtime is at 8:00 p.m."

I felt lucky to be left off, as this was my only chance to shop in Perugia. By the time we finished performing, all the shops would be closed, and we were leaving in the morning.

I dropped off my luggage in my room and quickly went downstairs. Stepping out of the hotel, I headed to the left, where I could see clothing shops. After all, how could I not shop for something Italian, given its fine materials, craftsmanship, and designs? I didn't have to walk far to find a shop with women's clothes, the only problem being whether I could afford anything in the store—and I only had a little time to decide.

As soon as I walked in, the clerk asked if she could help. I quickly explained that I only had a few minutes because I was a singer with the Mario Bauza band. Right away, she acknowledged knowing the band by saying, "Oh, hot mambo!"

The whole town was aware of many local artists participating in the music festival, where multiple acts would be playing simultaneously, some in auditoriums, others on outdoor stages in parks, and still others on small wooden stages in the side streets. For shop owners, it was a festival they eagerly anticipated, as it drew numerous tourists and many shoppers.

She quickly took me over to some scarves and explained how a beautiful scarf could dress up any simple dress, making an outfit look fabulous. Worried that I should have stayed in the hotel to rest, I agreed with her as she wrapped the item, and I was out and back in my room within forty-five minutes.

I really didn't have time to lie down. I had to take a shower and do my hair, which took some time. I was just about ready when the phone rang. The receptionist announced that my ride was waiting, and that I needed to come down quickly. I grabbed my makeup bag and headed out the door.

When I arrived, the band had just started, and after three numbers, it was my turn. Mario said, "Only one song because we're running behind." I was to sing the bolero, which I appreciated because, as I started singing, I could feel my body losing energy. I didn't realize how tired I was, but then I remembered I hadn't eaten anything that day.

I remember reading about Renée Fleming, the opera singer, and how she always carried a container of food because she couldn't sing on an empty stomach. Well, here I was, standing on stage, filling my diaphragm with air to sing out my high notes. Thankfully, I didn't miss a note. As I finished, the applause lifted me; otherwise, I might have passed out.

The show was great, as usual, but as we all boarded the bus, some musicians started complaining about how hungry they were. I, too, needed something to eat. The bus stopped at the musician's dining hall. I was lagging behind because some local singers wanted to take pictures and chat a bit. When I finally excused myself, I walked into the dining hall, only to see someone holding an empty tray that had contained tiramisu. Unfortunately, only wet crumbs and a little sauce were left. The server said all the food was gone and that they were just taking away the empty trays. Disappointed, I said, "Wait!" as I ran my fingers around the inside edge to scoop up the delicious coffee and cream sauce right into my mouth.

As I savored that one scoop, the server smiled and said, "You look hungry."

"Yes, indeed. So, where can I find something to eat?"

"Don't worry, walk down that way, and you'll find many places."

As I started walking, I could hear music coming from various sources, including the aroma of food. It was food that I wanted, so I let my nose lead the way when I heard my name: "Adelita!"

It was Victor Paz, the Panamanian trumpet player. "Come, I know a place where we can eat and hear some music."

He was like my savior, always watching out for me. We had a great time, enjoying ourselves and feeling pleased that we had made it to the end of the tour, having experienced many wonderful moments while visiting the different countries and cultures of Europe. The wonderful thing is that Europeans truly appreciate jazz and Latin jazz; as a result, many countries host festivals that bring in the best talent to entertain their jazz-loving audiences from around the world.

Finally, returning to New York City without any problems, we all dispersed to head home.

As soon as I walked in the door, Billy was waiting for me. He was happy to see me because he wanted to share his news. "I found a car!" he said excitedly.

It was a used BMW that the female owners offered to him at a reduced price because they fell in love with his story. The young man, a student at the Bronx High School of Science, working at Carmines, acting as the man of the house while his mother was away on tour—and not quite sixteen yet.

I gave him my pay from the tour, and though it was a lot of money, I was happy to provide it. After all, that's what mothers do, or at least this mother.

When you set out to see the cultural wonders of the world,
carry bread, cheese, cured ham, and local wine.
Culture is best experienced with all the senses.
You'll remember the sights, the tastes,
and the melodies long after.

CHAPTER 6

Tokyo With My First Recording

$\mathcal{M}$y room for a week was located on the upper floors of the tallest hotel in Tokyo. I had just returned to the room after spending the day with my Japanese record producer. We were following the promotional itinerary for the release of my first CD, *A Brazilian Affair*. It was a recording I had started a couple of years before, but had finally completed, printed, and published. Mr. P-San, my executive producer, wanted the recording for his label. He knew he could take the recording and promote it, knowing how much Brazilian and jazz music was appreciated not only by the Japanese in Japan, but also by the Japanese community in São Paulo, Brazil, which has approximately two million Japanese residents.

The promotional meetings were interesting and fun as we traveled around the city to various record stores. As I sat on the edge of the bed, I watched the traffic below moving swiftly as if the city itself had a pulse. It reminded me that this project, once slow and steady like my initial progress, was now moving faster than I had anticipated. I had to adjust, much like the cars racing through the streets—I needed to flow steadily, pushing forward no matter how quickly things seemed to change.

My mind floated in the web of my thoughts. Where could this take me? The excitement and anxiety tangled within me. It wasn't just a record anymore—it was a statement, a bridge between cultures. Every note, every rhythm, had to be as authentic as possible. After all, I was a Mexican American, a Chicana, channeling my passion for Brazilian music. When I first arrived in New York City, there wasn't much of a Chicano community to speak of. There were only two Mexican restaurants in the whole city. It wasn't until years later that Mexicans began to arrive in greater numbers, but even then, they weren't Mexican Americans. There were a couple of musicians from Arizona and New Mexico in our circle of friends, but I could count them on one hand. So, I joined the movement, influenced by the Brazilian artists of the time—Flora Purim and Tania Maria—who were carving out a new sound in the jazz world. Their music was a spark for me, and I couldn't help but be drawn to it.

The introduction of my music to the Brazilian community of Japanese was equally intriguing. The Japanese migration to Brazil began in the early twentieth century, when Brazilian laborers shifted to work in the mines for precious stones. Initially, the migration consisted of agriculture contracts lasting ten years, with the option to become citizens after completing them. As families grew, many Japanese immigrants invested their money in businesses, making Brazil their permanent home. My music, then, seemed a perfect fit—blending Brazilian rhythms with the jazz influences that had shaped me, and I could only hope it resonated with this unique community.

Brazilian music was already thriving in New York City and Europe with artists like Astrud Gilberto, the singer of "The Girl from Ipanema," and João Gilberto, who accompanied her alongside Stan Getz—who won a Grammy Award in 1965. Sergio Mendes and Brasil '66 also played a pivotal role, releasing a series of albums that blended American lyrics with Brazilian rhythms. In the 1970s, Flora Purim and Airto Moreira, both from *Return to Forever* with Chick Corea, helped further popularize Brazilian music in the United States. By the 1990s, this cultural movement was still going strong.

Various American singers have recorded Brazilian music, including Sarah Vaughan, Ella Fitzgerald, Frank Sinatra, and contemporary pop artists. It was Bebel Gilberto, the daughter of João Gilberto, who took things to a new level in the 2000s with her modern take on bossa nova. Her recordings brought Brazilian music back to the forefront. I was riding the wave of bossa nova music that I had fallen in love with, starting in the '80s, despite not being Brazilian, but working with Brazilian musicians. It felt fitting, and I loved the rhythm so much that I even learned to speak the language fluently.

One of the most memorable experiences of my journey was performing in Brazil with Brazilian pianist Aloisio Aguiar. We performed jazz standards with a bossa nova beat, a fusion that felt like the perfect expression of my musical identity. I was still mastering the Portuguese language, but performing alongside Aloisio allowed me to experience the culture in a way that words alone couldn't capture. The chance to practice Portuguese while ordering food, shopping, and chatting at small gatherings in his family's homes was invaluable. It was a vibrant, immersive experience—one that deepened my connection to Brazil in ways I hadn't anticipated.

Now, sitting comfortably perched on the inside ledge of the sizable picture window in my Tokyo hotel room, I reflected on my journey. Mr. P-San had offered me the opportunity to sing in his next production with saxophonist Lee Konitz. I was thrilled, as this was not only a chance to record my own albums, but also to collaborate with other legendary artists.

With my legs curled up and a notebook resting on my thighs, I stared out at the night sky, letting my thoughts drift. Below, I noticed the reflection of the moon shimmering in what appeared to be a small pond on the hotel grounds. For a moment, the stillness of the water mirrored my state of mind—quiet yet filled with a vision.

Inspired, I began to write. The lyrics came to me as if the moonlight itself had guided them. I imagined that the little pond was the ocean, and in my mind's eye, I saw a lonely girl walking along the beach, singing about her longing for love. As she sat on the sand, singing softly to herself, a falling star appeared overhead, and she made a wish—her heart's deepest desire: to love again.

Sad Love Song

Another night has fallen, and the moon is all aglow.
I can see her walking like so many nights before,
Stopping at her favorite spot—sitting on the sand
Singing sad songs about love,
Tears fall onto her hands.
A broken heart she cannot mend, although she tries again.
Singing songs of love, she starts to walk along the shore.
Suddenly, a falling star brightens up the sky,
Giving her a chance to mend her heart.

Oh, falling star, she sings tonight,
Her only wish—to give her one more chance to love.

And so, the night has fallen, and the moon is all aglow.
I can see her walking like so many nights before,
Stopping at her favorite spot, sitting on the sand,
Once again, she sings her sad love song.
La lala lala lala . . .

I was surprised by how easily the story formed into the lyrics that I would later present to Mr. Konitz, hoping he would agree to record it with me singing. However, that would have to wait until we returned to New York City. First, we had some promotional work to complete. The next day, Mr. P-San came to pick me up, and off we went to a couple of record shops to say hello and sign autographs at the displays of my CDs. It was a fun time walking to the locations through the busy city streets, occasionally stopping to admire the shops with outside displays of delicate tea sets and noodle bowls, each in numerous dainty patterns, all extremely attractive.

I let him lead the way, following behind him in the traditional Japanese manner of walking behind the men. Besides, I found it easier to navigate through the crowds depending on the time of day. After a couple of appointments, it was time for an early dinner. We arrived at a sushi bar where we sat at the *kaunta seki*—the counter seat where one can interact with the sushi chef. Mr. P-San placed an order, and soon a large bottle of Japanese beer arrived, accompanied by two glasses, which were gently placed in front of us. He explained that the female serves the drink to the male first, and then the male reciprocates.

I quickly recalled the many movie scenes of geishas singing while playing their stringed instruments or performing a dance with their beautiful hand-painted flower fans. I could almost picture the geishas, gracefully moving in tight silk kimonos, taking tiny steps toward their male guests, elegantly bending and shifting their knees to lower themselves into a sitting position. With artful elegance, she would lift the sake flask with her poised hands to serve the drink. I snapped out of my thoughts and, with the same grace, gently reached with both hands to lift the bottle. I poured the beer and carefully replaced the bottle, as Mr. P-San smiled and then poured my glass.

Next, the chef passed me a small *geta*—a wooden tray—with a carefully toasted spine of a small two-inch eel, topped with a tiny sprinkle of crushed rock salt. As the chef bowed, he said, "Calcium for woman."

I thought, *How considerate.* I truly appreciated it and enjoyed the moment because, back home, whenever I opened a can of sardines or salmon, I would always eat the spine before breaking the fish up to make a sandwich. While the spine doesn't have much taste, it's more about the texture of the bone that gets crushed between your teeth.

As the two men watched, I carefully took the spine between my chopsticks and placed it on my tongue. I closed my mouth and bit down gently, as femininely as possible, thinking, *How would the geishas have done it?*

Then, a tray with two shrimp came my way. I could see the ten-gallon fish tank behind the chef, with a small net that he used to capture the eel and the shrimp. They couldn't be any fresher unless the chef scooped it out of a body of water behind the restaurant. He carefully placed the live shrimp head down. He removed the shell, leaving the bit of meat of the tail intact. There it was, with the tail pointing up to the ceiling. I watched, intrigued by how the chef managed to place the shrimp in this position without it falling over. The head of the shrimp was making a few bubbling sounds.

"Oh no, it's alive!" I cried.

I know sushi is eaten fresh in Japan, typically brought to the restaurant that morning from the fish markets, but would I dare eat a shrimp that was still gasping?

They explained that it was only a bit of water still finding its way out of the body, as it was upside down.

Again, the chef and Mr. P-San gestured for me to take the first bite, encouraging me to grab the head with my chopsticks and bite off the body. I grabbed the head, still making those bubbling sounds, and said, "Well, here it goes."

Into my mouth it went. I bit down and chewed gently. The shrimp was sweet, tender, and almost seemed to melt in my mouth. I took another bite, this time ignoring the hissing sound of the shrimp.

The meal continued with sushi, sashimi, and some special hand rolls, all while we talked about the schedule for the next couple of days.

As we headed back to the hotel, it was just after 6:00 p.m.—rush hour, with people streaming out of work. Mr. P-San pointed me in the direction of the hotel, just two blocks away. He explained that he needed to rush off but would meet me again tomorrow for the remaining appointments on the itinerary.

As I reached the next corner, I saw what looked like a wall of men heading straight towards me. I was shocked to see so many men my height, all with dark, straight hair parted to the side, walking in unison like an army of soldiers. They were all dressed in white shirts, dark suits, and matching dark ties. I thought to myself, *Are they going to knock me down? Walk over me?*

Clearly, they were heading to the train station I had just passed. I stood still, thinking, *I'll just stay put and let them go around me.* And sure enough, they did. The wall of men parted as if by design, splitting open to allow those walking to the left and right pass without ever bumping into me.

I've got to say, it was a little scary, almost surreal.

The next day I had the morning off, so I went for a walk since the lyrics were now completed. The hotel was located near the Imperial Palace, which spans over 800 acres in the heart of Tokyo and serves as the residence of the emperor and his family. The original Edo Castle, built in 1457, featured several defensive stone walls and moats. However, it was destroyed during World War II in 1945 and subsequently rebuilt into the magnificent palace it is today. Unfortunately, tourists aren't allowed to visit the palace unless they are dignitaries on official government business. However, I did have the chance to walk along one side of the gated property. Along the way, I spotted a couple of small Shinto shrines before continuing my mission to find a banana, which I was craving.

I arrived at a lively shopping area with colorful shops lining both sides of the road. Foot traffic was steady, with women strolling by with their shopping baskets casually hung over their arms. As I walked, I spotted a small row of bright yellow bananas neatly arranged in bunches of five or six, surrounded by other perfectly shiny, unblemished fruit. I leaned over to grab a bunch, intending to break off a single banana, but the shop-keeper was quick to notice my intentions. Before I could do anything, he snatched the bunch out of my hands and said firmly, "No!"

I pointed to myself, then to the bananas, saying, "No, I only want one banana."

Once again, he repeated, "No!"

Well, I wasn't going to buy a bunch when I only wanted one banana. I would be leaving Tokyo before I could finish the bunch, and besides, when I looked at the price, I couldn't afford to buy a whole bunch. I looked at the shopkeeper with his grim face, then I looked around the shop and realized it was a high-priced gourmet shop with very carefully hand-picked items for his clientele, of whom I was not.

My shopping adventure had come to an end, and dark clouds were starting to gather overhead. It was time to get back to the hotel without a banana to prepare for the day's appointments before the rain began. When Mr. P-San arrived, he said we would take the subway, because traffic got worse when it rained. So, there I was, once again following behind him, holding up my umbrella, which I quickly closed as we joined the crowd streaming down the stairs, entering the subway station.

Of course, as expected, it was crowded, and it was amusing to watch when the subway car doors opened. People rushed into the empty cars, and once they were completely full, attendants holding a long, thick rod would stop anyone else from squeezing in. They used the rod to help push the people further in so the doors could close.

An even funnier sight was a long bench of people asleep, leaning on one another. Apparently, no one minds—everyone needs a shoulder to catch a few extra winks. The working class can't afford to live in the city, so they commute from the outer suburbs, enduring long hours at work and lengthy train rides. They seize any moment to snooze.

The early evening still offered raindrops off and on, but it was dinnertime. In his broken English, Mr. P-San said, "No sushi today. Never when the sea is rough. Today, is *Udon-ya* in *zashiki* restaurant."

The noodle restaurant's décor was all-wood, with dining rooms furnished with low wooden tables, each surrounded by four to eight zabuton cushions and a recessed footwell for comfort. The delicate sliding shoji screens completed the look, while the sound of a soft Japanese Koto harp set the atmosphere, allowing one to forget the rainy evening.

The warm soup arrived at the table, brought by the waitress wearing a casual, flowery-patterned kimono of peonies, pine trees, and several small white cranes—symbols of good fortune scattered across the fabric. The steam rising from the broth gave off just enough warmth to invite me to lean forward, letting the warmth gently touch my nose, which still carried a little chill from walking in the rain.

As we began to eat, I noticed Mr. P-San began slurping his noodles up from the bowl and into his puckered mouth. Of course, I had seen this many times in Japanese TV shows and movies, but I wasn't raised with the slurping technique.

Mr. P-San encouraged me to slurp right along with him, but it's not easy if you're not accustomed to it. The trick is not to shower your clothes with soup while sucking up the noodles. I continued to eat as I usually would. It was delicious, and it warmed off the dampness that had clung to the rest of my body.

As I continued eating, I thought about how glad I was that the schedule was completed. I was ready to get back home and get back to work. An artist never stops—there's always something to do. After all, I had a new CD out, so there were many details to manage in preparation for the upcoming performance. I was also eager to present my lyrics to Lee Konitz for his recording session.

The next day, I had a breakfast of grilled salmon, a green salad, and warm porridge, and grabbed the banana I had been craving. Afterward, I returned to my room to pack my bags and wait for Mr. P-San to pick me up. It was teatime when he arrived. He instructed me to leave my luggage with the concierge and that we would return for it later.

He took me to a quaint little tea shop with four small tables for two, each with delicate teacup settings. The waitress poured the tea and brought us some French-style pastries, including tarts made with Japanese ingredients like green matcha and black sesame, along with tarts so delicate-looking that I almost didn't want to destroy the fine, small works of art by crushing them in my mouth. But, of course, it would have been silly not to taste as many as they offered.

Then I was off to the airport after the beautiful experience of having French style pastries in a Japanese tea house as the finishing touch of my trip. With an armful of presents, I very carefully carried my gifts from Mr.

P-San, a tea set and some handsome noodle bowls, along with a couple of tubes filled with my promotional picture posters, all the way back to NYC.

When in Japan, adjust the sound of your
voice—even a baby's cry is quiet.

CHAPTER 7

A Drink on the Nile

was performing at Birdland Jazz Club on 52nd Street in New York City back in 2004, when a group of friends came backstage to say hello. Among them was the Egyptian ambassador, carrying a bouquet of sweet, pink, fragrant roses. He was smiling ear to ear, holding out the bouquet as he said, "Ah, la crème Latina. I'm so happy to meet you."

I thought, *He's calling me the name of one of my CDs.* He continued, "I have been one of your fans since I discovered your music."

I thought, *Wonderful, a fan that belongs on the VIP list of backstage invites.* Then he said, "Our tourist director would like to invite you, along with some journalists, on a junket to visit the pyramids. It also includes a cruise along the Nile River to explore our most important historic attractions. It's a trip that begins in Cairo, followed by a local flight to the city of Aswan. The tour continues up the Nile on a small cruise boat, making important historic stops along the way. We ask that the invited writers document their journey to help promote the beauty of Egypt."

I immediately felt the tiny butterflies in my tummy wake up and flutter their wings. I could also feel the ears of my closest groupies perk up. I glanced around and saw eyeballs starting to roll toward us. The words *travel* and *Egypt* could catch anyone's attention.

Then we all heard, "We would like to include you on this tour to perform for us at the El Sawy Culture Wheel at the end of the journey. We have a wonderful group of musicians who can accompany you at the center."

I was stunned by such an exciting offer, and so were my friends. I could already picture myself packing my lightweight clothes, because I understood how hot it could get in Egypt. But you can't believe any offer 100 percent until the travel agent calls asking for your picture and passport number.

I counted to seven silently so I wouldn't sound too anxious about the opportunity. "Yes, I'd love to go!" I replied.

I recalled that the longest flight I'd ever been on was to Singapore, to perform at the Thundering Drums Festival. That trip was seventeen hours long, with one stop, twelve hours in, landing in Germany to refuel before continuing to Singapore. Egypt would be a twelve-hour flight from New York City—not bad in comparison.

I'd been waiting months to hear back from the tourist office so we could coordinate the tour. Finally, the call came, and the itinerary arrived in the mail. As I read through it, I saw that we'd have an additional night's stay at a hotel near the tip of Mount Sinai in the heart of Sharm el-Sheikh—a resort town that hugs the Red Sea. I had never heard of Sharm el-Sheikh before, and the Red Sea, to me, was just a body of water bordering Saudi Arabia and Egypt. It all felt so foreign, but I was excited. It was going to be a very educational trip, and I'd get to perform.

I never considered exploring the political tensions in the area. It was 2005, and the world seemed to have more security in place by then. Besides, I wasn't really paying attention to world news. I was focused on music and art. When you're young, who has time for distractions when you're fully engaged in your profession and enjoying life?

The tour was government-sponsored, so we would have security with us at all times. At the end of the cruise, we'd return to Cairo, where the group would then fly back to NYC. I, however, would stay a few extra days to rehearse and perform before heading home. I could hardly wait.

The day finally arrived. I was at the airport, greeting the writers on the junket as they introduced themselves. Everyone was excited to be part of this small, select group. The only male among us was an expedition archaeologist. The rest were female: a photojournalist, three writers, and I.

On the long twelve-hour flight, I tried to sleep as much as I could, knowing I'd want to take advantage of every moment once we landed in Cairo.

The wheels of the very comfortable, government-owned EgyptAir flight finally touched down. We were met by government security personnel and our tour guide, Omar, who would accompany us at all times when we were in public.

We stepped into a large passenger van and began the ride from the airport into downtown Cairo. Omar explained the presence of our two bodyguards, introduced us to our driver, and reassured us that they would be with us throughout the trip for our safety.

At first, all we could see was golden sand glowing under the bright, glaring sun. A few cars dotted the road leading us away from the airport, which was quiet and not very busy. As we continued, the gilded heat of the sand began to give way to green vegetation—the result of irrigation canals fed by the Nile River. Both sides of the river supported rich agriculture, and the land was planted with crops along the banks.

As we moved along, we entered the outer limits of central Cairo. The number of cars increased along the long green arms of the river, which gave way to gray apartment buildings, with no painted bricks, just concrete blocks, and not a single palm tree in sight. Then, slowly, we moved into an area of commerce, which was busy, bustling, and full of life.

Looking out the window, we traveled along the Sixth of October Bridge—a bridge dedicated to the soldiers of the Yom Kippur War (1973). This conflict eventually led to Egypt regaining control of the Sinai Peninsula from Israel. Below, I saw large groups of people gathered, many of whom were wearing their traditional attire. I leaned forward, curious about the scene, and asked, "Is there a festival going on?"

Our tour guide, Omar, was quick to respond, his English clear and confident. "Street space is limited in Cairo," he said. "There's plenty of open desert outside the city limits—but it's only good if you own a camel."

The group laughed, and Omar continued, "There are very few gathering places like parks or open public spaces. We have many street vendors that take up the sidewalks, and people gather while waiting for transportation. It also serves as our social space."

So, no, it was not a festival, but rather a daily gathering of people going through their daily motions.

We arrived at the hotel, and before we got off the bus, Omar reminded us of our dinner plans and offered to take anyone to the bazaar before it got too late to walk and shop. Ann, the photojournalist, and I accepted his offer. The others decided to rest before meeting again for dinner, where we'd watch the Tanoura dancers perform with their colorful twirling skirts on a riverboat nearby on the Nile.

The Nile River originates at Lake Victoria, situated in East Central Africa—one of the largest tropical lakes in the world, and the second-largest freshwater lake after Lake Superior in the United States. From there, it flows north, cutting through the heart of Cairo, before finally merging with the waters of the Mediterranean Sea.

Once we arrived at the bazaar, we walked along long, narrow corridors of paved paths, with side streets curving off in different directions. We passed tables of men smoking flavorful shisha (hookah) and sipping tea, their eyes following us as we went by. A young child ran up to me, offering wooden snakes for a few nickels. Sweet, attractive scents filled the air as we passed perfumed oil shops, with handsome shopkeepers standing proudly outside their storefronts, trying to lure us in.

If Ann or I wandered off, one of the security agents would always be nearby, keeping a watchful eye to ensure we were safe, waiting patiently if we stepped into a shop, or gently suggesting we avoid certain side streets. Being young and naive to the potential dangers I might encounter, it gave me a quiet peace of mind knowing he was always just a few steps behind me.

We continued walking past herbal shops and tables stacked with brightly colored spices shaped into small pyramids. Their aromas mixed, dancing in the air around us.

My first encounter with a public bathroom in the bazaar was surprisingly appreciated. It was immaculate, with a plain, functional décor. The walls were unpainted cement with simple fixtures, and instead of a bidet, like you'd find in many European countries or Argentina, there was a water hose. I was given toilet paper upon entering, but simply having the chance to refresh myself was a delight.

We were eventually lured into a perfume shop, where we received what felt like diplomatic treatment—they served us tea and biscuits with a warmth that made us feel honored. Looking back now, I suspect it had been prearranged by the travel agent, knowing someone in our group would be eager to explore the bazaar as soon as possible. After all, we were tourists, and every tourist dollar counts.

I managed to treat myself to a small bottle of perfumed oil called *Egyptian Flowers*. It was heavenly. I still have a bit left in the bottle, which I've stretched by adding a little mineral oil to reclaim its scent.

When we stepped out of the shop, I spotted our security guard, Mohamed, standing nearby in his dark grey suit, his strong physique giving him a commanding presence. All of our communication had gone through Omar—I never heard a word from Mohamed. Then again, no one in our group spoke Arabic.

I had learned that Egypt was always on alert since its last peace treaty with Israel. Depending on what's happening in the world, the flow of tourists can shift, which in turn affects the country's tourism economy. Many countries that don't produce enough goods for export rely heavily on tourism, and protecting those cities becomes essential to avoid any threats that could harm the industry.

Traveling around the world, I've seen police officers stationed on street corners, but it's the plainclothes guards you don't see that often who offer the most substantial presence. Over time, I developed a kind of rule of thumb for my own peace of mind: if I see a police officer, I feel safe. If I see soldiers standing guard, that's high alert. And if I see soldiers with automatic rifles, that's very high alert, and it's time to go home. It's smart to stay observant. But for the most part, tourists are safe as long as they don't stray too far off the beaten path.

We returned to the hotel just in time to get dressed for dinner, which was to be held on a boat docked across the Nile—the same one I could see from my hotel window. It was a floating restaurant with a floor show where we would get to see the famous twirling Tanoura dancers. I had heard about their colorful skirts spinning like kaleidoscopes.

By the time we arrived, the band had just finished their set. Adrianna, the singer for the evening's show, came over to introduce herself. She'd been told that an American group was coming to the restaurant and that a singer among them would soon be performing at the El Sawy Culture Wheel.

She was Italian, gorgeous, tall, and spoke several languages. We settled on Portuguese. She shared that her contract at the restaurant would be ending soon and that she was hoping for an opportunity to move to New York City. She said she'd love to come to my show, but unfortunately, she had to work the same night. Very understandable; Friday and Saturday nights were our busiest nights as performers.

I gladly gave her my business card (it was still the thing to do back then). I never heard from her, but I still think about Adrianna, *la cantante*.

After dinner, and after the dizzying, hypnotic floor show performed by the twirling dancers in the Sufi tradition, we returned to the hotel. We said our goodnights, buzzing with excitement for the next day's journey. I would have liked to have stayed a while longer to keep talking with Adrianna, maybe even meet the members of her band, but we were on the government's security schedule, and that meant it was time to head back. We had an early wake-up call to see the pyramids.

I got ready for bed, and as soon as my head hit the pillow, I was out like Sleeping Beauty. But not for long.

I woke to the smell of smoke. Startled, I got up and looked around the room. I checked the bathroom and carefully put my hand on the bedroom door before opening it, but the smell was strongest inside the room.

Then I heard the beeping of car horns below that sounded musical—taxi drivers communicating amongst themselves, tapping like in an Egyptian Morse code.

I pulled the curtains open. The beeping grew louder. When I opened the window, I realized what it was—not fire, but pollution. The night air was thick. I could see the haze glowing against the lights of a nearby bridge off to the left.

And then, slightly to the right, shining along the Nile River, was the boat where we'd had dinner. It was lit up and festive, still alive with music and light.

Straight ahead, through the haze, I spotted the Cairo Tower, a 614-foot structure considered a national symbol of pride in Egypt. It stood tall, its latticework design inspired by the lotus plant, which in ancient Egyptian culture represented purity and rebirth. There was a restaurant and an observation deck at the top, and I'd been told that on a clear day, you could see the pyramids from there.

Once I understood the lay of the land—and that the smoky smell was just the thick night air of Cairo—I settled down again. As tired as I was, I had no problem falling back asleep, even with the stirring thought that in the morning, we would be visiting the pyramids.

It was something I had never imagined seeing in person.

THE PYRAMIDS AND THE SPHINX

I woke to the phone ringing in my ear—my wake-up call. I got up quickly and pulled the curtains open. The view was bathed in full sun. In the morning light, I could clearly see the lotus design on the Cairo Tower—the same structure I had strained to see through the haze the night before.

Knowing how hot it would get, I grabbed my white, lightweight gauze scarf, which could serve as protection from the sun or cover my head and shoulders if needed for cultural respect. I dressed quickly and made my way down to breakfast.

I sat with the group in the hotel's dining room as we shared our first impressions, mainly about the ever-present beeping of the cars and the heavy smell of smoke in the air. We had all experienced the same sensory surprise.

The van was waiting for us outside. We all climbed in—our driver, bodyguards, Omar, and all six of us in the group. It was the first day we really had a chance to talk among ourselves, to warm up a bit and settle into our shared experience.

I struck up a conversation with the archaeologist once I learned he was from Argentina. That gave us something in common, and I was naturally curious since I had never met an archaeologist before. We spoke in Spanish, as it was easier for him, and by the time we arrived at the pyramids forty-five minutes later, we had become friends.

I also got to know Sofia, the "mother" of the group, who was older than I was. She carried herself with a certain grace and confidence, offering guidance and knowledge as we went. She was an experienced writer on a mission: she was hoping to interview one of Egypt's most well-known personalities, the archaeologist Dr. Zahi Hawass.

Meeting him wasn't on our itinerary, but she was hopeful that his schedule might open up. I knew exactly who he was; he was a familiar face on US television at the time, hosting shows about excavations in the Valley of the Kings along the Nile River. He was also promoting the King Tutankhamun exhibit at the Egyptian Museum in Cairo while we were there, though unfortunately, that too wasn't on our itinerary—we'd been told there simply wasn't enough time to fit it in.

The two younger girls bonded easily; they were close in age, and both were ambitious young writers, always with notebooks in hand, constantly scribbling thoughts and impressions. The photojournalist had her own agenda, snapping pictures quietly, rarely chatting, always seeing the world through her lens.

We crossed the Nile River, passed through Cairo, and entered Giza, heading to the far west side where the sand meets the great pyramids. As we approached, the pyramids began to rise before us, growing larger with every mile. They looked just as they do in pictures, on TV, in books, and magazines, but to see them in person was another thing entirely. One of the true wonders of the world, and yes, they were truly impressive.

Omar was quick to point out the three smaller pyramids, referred to as the "Queens' Pyramids." I hadn't remembered those from school. I thought to myself, *Did our schoolbooks even mention them?* Only one of the three, the tomb of Queen Khentkawes, remains intact. It's believed to have been built taller than the others to serve not only as her tomb, but also as a tribute. She was the wife of Pharaoh Sneferu, the second ruler of Egypt.

There were so many facts shared with us, too many to retain all at once. I took in what I could, knowing I wouldn't remember every name, but grateful we'd been given reference books to take home.

There was a lot to learn.

By this point, we were ready to enter the largest of the pyramids—that of Pharaoh Sneferu. A small line had formed outside to begin the climb up the wooden stairs. The air was dry and heavy. After what felt like endless steps, there was a narrow landing where one person could sit to catch their breath or wipe the sweat from their brow. The heat built up quickly from the climb and the enclosed space.

Finally, we reached the upper chamber—a large, dim room containing only a cement sarcophagus. People were quietly taking turns stepping inside for the experience. I was curious and took my turn.

The sarcophagus was about three feet deep. I climbed in, lay down, and closed my eyes. Instantly, I was surrounded by the darkest black I'd ever seen. It startled me. A fear swept over me, sudden and sharp. I opened my eyes and quickly sat up. I felt claustrophobic, like I had made a mistake, like I shouldn't have gotten in at all. I headed down quickly, asking a few people to let me cut the line to get out.

Once I stepped out into the brightness of the sunlight, I thought, *Boy, that was dumb. What was the point of that experience?* But with the warm sun on my face, the fear quickly vanished.

Sofia came out next and asked if I was alright. She noticed I'd left so quickly and hadn't waited for anyone in the group. Just then, the younger girls emerged and came over to us, excitedly asking where they could ride a camel.

I wanted to ride a camel too . . . or at least sit on one and get a photo. But I wasn't going to spend the money. Sofia, however, took the lead. We followed her as she approached one of the camel masters and asked about the price, which was too high.

I was on a very tight budget. I'd already spent more than I should have at the bazaar the day before, and the Nile cruise hadn't even started yet.

Sofia was a champ; totally fearless when it came to bargaining. I pulled her aside and said, "No, don't bother. I'm saving my money for the cruise."

She looked at me with that spark in her eye and said, "Come on. You want a picture on the camel, don't you?"

"But he wants too much," I replied, raising my voice to match hers.

By now, we were attracting attention, and the camel master watched us, a little amused, as we went back and forth. "Just pull out five dollars," Sofia said. "All you want is the picture, don't you?"

Then, turning and calling up to the man, she shouted, "Let her on! All she wants is the picture. You don't have to take her anywhere!"

She said it in a loud, nervy voice, not giving him a chance to say no.

"Just bring the camel down so she can get on. Come on, she just wants the picture!" Sofia insisted, waving her arm.

A minute later, the camel slowly began bending its knees, lowering itself with that signature groaning motion so I could climb on. *Ah*, I thought, *this is why they ask for fifteen dollars. Just getting the camel to sit is a task.*

The next moment, the camel was back up on its feet, and I was sitting behind its handsome master, waving for the camera as Sofia snapped the photo. I was so happy. Of course, I wanted the picture! People back home were bound to ask if I rode a camel and got the photo. Well, I didn't get the ride, but I got to sit on top of one, behind a very photogenic guide. And I had my picture.

The whole moment was fun; pure chaos that Sofia stirred up, and somehow, it worked.

From there, we walked over to the mighty Sphinx. The area was clearly still under excavation in places. What struck me most was how close the Giza neighborhood sat, just across a street from the sand where the park and monuments began. I could understand why there was such tight security. If I lived there, I might be tempted to start digging, too, just to see what I could find. I imagined someone with the right tools going deep into their backyard—but then again, where would they even put all that sand?

When we reached the front of the Sphinx, it struck me as even larger than I'd imagined. It created an illusion, maybe because of its placement or the way it loomed against the flat desert landscape. It was actually easier to get a photo with the Sphinx than it was with the camel.

Next up was lunch at Cheristo Seafood Restaurant, one of the locals' favorites. We sat out on the terrace, with the pyramids standing in the background. By the time I took my seat, my back was to them. I was the last to sit, so I didn't get the best view. But honestly, I was more focused on food at that point.

I ordered a grilled fish and chatted with Santiago while we waited. We compared notes on our experiences with the pyramid. He had gone into the second pyramid and said it was a totally different interior—you descend instead of climbing up. He didn't seem too thrilled with it; he said it wasn't anything special. So, it sounded like a different experience altogether—one I didn't get to see, so I guess it was no loss.

As we continued talking, Santiago leaned in and said, "No miras pa'trás." *Don't look back.*

Apparently, there was a table of men nearby, sipping tea and smoking shisha, speaking among themselves and glancing our way. I had noticed them briefly before sitting down.

"They seem to be looking and talking about you," Santiago added.

I turned to look, and sure enough, all eyes were on me.

"They're probably just trying to figure out what my ethnicity is," I said, casually.

I've got one of those faces and that tone of skin that can blend in a lot of places. It happens often—people wonder where I'm from.

Then the food arrived, and I was delighted to see an entire grilled fish, head and tail still intact, perfectly cooked and served with halved lemons. Every morsel was delicious.

"They're definitely still talking about you," Santiago said with a grin.

I turned around again and, with a little smile, called out, "I'm *Latina!*"

Suddenly, the curious faces turned into smiling ones, heads nodding up and down and hands going up in the air. It seemed like someone at that table had guessed correctly. I couldn't help but wonder who won the bet.

THE CRUISE

By late afternoon, we were boarding a short one-and-a-half-hour flight south to Aswan to begin our journey on the Nile. We arrived with just enough time to check into our rooms and shower before dinner on the deck.

With only six people in our group, plus Omar and our security crew, each of us had a private room, complete with our own attendant who kept everything immaculate and was available on call for any request.

We were aboard a typical boat used for Nile cruising, known as a *Dahabiya*. Ours was a modern version—motorized, so it didn't need a tugboat to dock. The sail was not engaged, as I was told they mainly used it for show. If you want to get somewhere sooner, you use the motor. Still, the atmosphere was peaceful, with an unhurried pace; no lines, no crowds, and no loud chatter.

My room—berth number four—was bright and inviting, with soft pastel-patterned wallpaper, dark wood accents, and windows that let in the golden light. The bed was especially cozy, with a good mattress that made me feel instantly at home.

A fresh basket of sweet pastries and fruit greeted me as I stepped inside. I had just enough time for a forty-five-minute nap before dinner in the dining room.

When I arrived (once again, the last to sit), I found myself facing the west bank of the Nile. It was already dark outside. I'd have to wait until morning to start spotting the bunches of dates on the palms, something my neighbor back home had told me to look out for when I mentioned my trip to Egypt.

At dinner, we shared our excitement about the wonders ahead: temples, ancient cities, and life along the river. The conversation was light and full of anticipation.

When I returned to my cabin after dinner, I noticed the snack tray had been refreshed with delicate pastries—flaky layers filled with almonds, pistachios, and sweetened with honey—along with a pot of fresh mint tea.

No after-dinner drinks were served, as alcohol wasn't available on our boat. But that didn't bother me. I was a tea drinker, and a pot of mint tea under the stars on the Nile felt just right.

ASWAN AND THE TEMPLE OF ISIS

The morning breakfast moved quickly as we headed off to visit the Temple of Isis—also known as the Philae Temple—dedicated to the goddess Isis, who is associated with magic, motherhood, fertility, and love.

Omar filled our minds with ancient stories, including the myth of how Isis collected the scattered parts of her brother Osiris's body after their other brother dismembered him, and how she used her magic to bring him back to life. I confirmed with Omar that the story of Isis was indeed one of the most widely celebrated across many cultures throughout the Mediterranean region.

As we walked toward the temple complex and got closer, the structures appeared massive, larger than expected. Some of the carvings looked almost freshly etched, as though they had been made only decades ago, not thousands of years before.

In 2004, when I visited, the major restoration project (which began in 2019) hadn't started yet, so I was seeing the temple in its original, time-worn form. Some of the walls were too delicate to touch, and shouldn't be touched, with the winds constantly contributing to their slow deterioration.

I noticed how the reliefs and etchings had been carved first, then assembled block by block, aligning each figure as best as possible. If you looked closely, you could see where parts of a figure didn't perfectly match from one stone to the next. The imperfect alignment only highlighted the painstaking work of the artisans; it had to take years, maybe lifetimes, of labor to create something so magnificent.

Several of the columns in the inner court still bore the original lotus flower motif, opened in full bloom. The lotus, I learned, symbolized creation and rebirth because it is a flower that sinks into muddy waters at night, only to rise again, cleansed, to face the sun each morning in all its glory.

It had been an informative, fascinating, and very warm day. I'm not sure what the temperature was, but I was more than ready to head back to the boat, where I could drink plenty of cool water. I couldn't wait to step into a refreshing shower before having some lunch and then a well-earned nap.

By dinnertime, we were already on our way to our next stop, set to arrive by morning. I fell asleep going over the lyrics to the songs I'd be performing at the show in Cairo, the soft rumble of the boat's motor keeping time like a metronome. The gentle rocking helped, too.

TEMPLE OF KOM OMBO

I had forgotten to close the shades, so the sunlight woke me. When I looked out the window, I was staring straight into the window of another boat. I didn't understand what was going on.

I quickly got ready and headed to the breakfast room, where I asked why we were docked next to another vessel. Sofia was quick to explain.

"To get out to the landing, you'll have to walk through the other boats lined up. This is a very popular stop, and there's limited room at the dock. The boats moor side by side, allowing guests to pass through each one until they reach the ramp. Just keep your ID handy—each boat has its own concierge, and you'll need to show it when entering and exiting. Additionally, we'll be approached by numerous vendors. You might want to bring a little money in case you see something you like."

I thought, *well, I already have my perfume oil, a snake, and a Sphinx.* I was saving up for a full-size painting on papyrus paper. Still, I was prepared because you never know what you might find.

I was incredibly grateful for this trip, as all expenses were covered while in Egypt, yet I still kept a close eye on my budget. I was more interested in bringing money home than leaving it behind. After all, I had bills waiting for me the moment I stepped through my apartment door.

Oh well, for now, it was time to see the next temple.

We had arrived in the town of Kom Ombo. Omar was already nearby, advising us to stay within his sight because of the crowds. I could already see the Temple of Kom Ombo as soon as I stepped onto the ramp.

As I walked up, I got distracted by the many vendors standing just outside their stalls on the sidewalk before the stairs that led to the temple. There must be a law preventing them from stepping more than a foot onto the concrete walkway so that they wouldn't block the path of potential shoppers.

If you looked down the row, you'd see a very colorful display of clothes hanging neatly, with some vendors holding up a garment, ready to help you decide which color looked best. I thought, *No shopping for me,* and headed up the stairs.

There it was—a large, symmetrical structure. Like the temples we had already seen, it had missing walls and columns adorned with the now-familiar lotus flower design, which wrapped around the tops and held up the heavy stone roof.

Kom Ombo is unique, Omar explained, because it's a double temple—one half dedicated to Sobek, the crocodile god, and the other to Haroeris (Horus the Elder), the falcon god. Each side had its own sanctuaries and halls, a mirror image of the other, honoring both deities equally.

As I stood there in the dry heat, I wondered: With so much sun, did they even *have* many walls? Maybe they hung light linen curtains for privacy, allowing the breeze to pass through. The stone etchings depicted stories of ancient Egyptians, but I wasn't listening too closely to Omar, I was reviewing my lyrics in my head.

At the same time, I imagined people from thousands of years ago walking through those same entrances, wearing sandals made of braided papyrus stalks, palm leaves, or perhaps leather from cows. I wondered, *Cows—what prehistoric animal did they evolve from?* Crocodile leather, I figured, was probably reserved for royalty and used in belts and sandals, and maybe even eaten on rare occasions.

The clothing for women would be a *kalasiris,* as seen in the hieroglyphics—a simple sheath dress with one or two straps over the shoulders. Men would wrap themselves in soft linen, creating the *shendyt,* a type of skirt.

All this thinking was making me hungry. Fortunately, I had wrapped a few snacks and found a shady spot to sit and eat. I was shaking the last drop of water from my bottle into my mouth when Sofia came over to join me. A couple of tourists from another group sitting nearby struck up a conversation. They were a lovely couple and shared some of their experiences so far. I thought, *It's nice when you get to mingle with like-minded people on a trip—it makes everything more memorable.*

I looked around and noticed that the crowd had thinned out. Sam and Charles had left, and Sofia and I were still chatting.

With the sun finally out of my eyes, I asked Sofia to take my picture. We were done. She said, "Let's go find some food. I want to ask if they secured my appointment with Mr. Hawass."

TEMPLE OF HORUS

Our next stop was to see one of the best-preserved temples in all of Egypt, which was dedicated to the falcon-headed deity, Horus. He was associated with the sun through his right eye and the moon through his left. As a result, Horus represented protection, healing, and power. According to mythology, Horus was the son of Isis. After Isis's brother murdered her husband Osiris, she used her magic to resurrect Osiris and later gave birth to Horus, who avenged his father's death.

The structure and the surrounding grounds were impressive, not only for their scale but for how well they've endured. The exterior walls are adorned with vivid carvings that recount the mythological tale of Horus and his rise to power as a revered ruler and protector.

Egyptian history is rich not only in its line of real-life pharaohs but also in its pantheon of deities. Each god and goddess represents a powerful concept: nature and its forces, cosmic order and morality, death and the afterlife, kingship and divine rule, fertility, love, protection, and the potent magic of healing and knowledge.

With so much history layered into each temple, it's no wonder that official government tour guides must undergo extensive education. Their knowledge, especially of the narratives carved into these sacred walls, helps bring Egypt's incredible past to life.

CRUISING ON THE NILE

We were headed next toward Luxor with a full day of cruising on the Nile. Lunch was served on deck with a variety of dishes. I filled my plate and sat down with the group. As usual, I was the last one to come up from my room, and everyone had already served themselves. As I sat down, one of the young girls asked if I had helped myself to the little legs being offered. I looked down at my plate. "Yes, they may be frog legs, which I had eaten once before in New York," I told them. They looked at me curiously as I looked again more closely. "No, they look like pigeon legs. I heard they eat pigeon here, like in some other countries in the world," I said as I ate the small legs, which were very interesting, not bad.

I looked over at Omar, who was standing by a rail, drinking something dark red.

"Omar, what are you drinking that looks so inviting?"

"Karkade, it's delicious. You want to try?"

"Sure."

Omar served me a glass of the tea. When I tasted it, I liked the tart, bitter taste once the rich, too sugary taste dissipated.

I asked the waiter for half a glass of water. I added the tea to the water to reduce the overly sweet taste. Everyone watched me and asked how it was. "Delightful and refreshing," I said.

They all wanted to try it, so I asked Omar to have the kitchen make a pitcher with half the sugar and to add more water. We all ended up drinking *Karkade* the rest of the trip.

It wasn't until I visited my mother in Texas, months after I returned, that I made another surprising discovery. She was going to make mole sauce for my favorite dish—enchiladas. She instructed me to go to the produce section of the grocery store, where I would find a stack of wooden crates filled with various types of chiles. I found the stack and began sifting through it, starting from the top. I reached the midway point when she called out, "Those aren't chiles. Those are hibiscus flowers."

I looked at the side of the crate and saw that it was marked 'Jamaica.' I thought, *That's strange that they'd have these dry flowers next to the chiles. Surely, they made a mistake.* When I returned home and told my mother what I had found, she laughed and explained, "Pues sí, it's the red agua fresca you see at the taco stands in big jars, right alongside pineapple juice, horchata (rice water with cinnamon and vanilla), and the flor de Jamaica water." Ah, it was the same flower water in Egypt—or *karkade*.

I had no idea. Whenever I spotted the fresh Mexican waters at taco stands, I had always assumed the red drink was strawberry. I preferred limeade, so I never paid much attention. However, I have now learned that Jamaica and Egypt both produce hibiscus flowers for tea.

We all lingered on the deck, taking pictures and watching the sails of the feluccas on the river. They looked so peaceful. I started counting the palm trees along the riverbank, spotting the bunches of dates hanging from them. At moments, I thought about Elizabeth Taylor and Richard Burton, imagining the wonderful time they must have had on the Nile River during their off days from filming. Their romance was legendary, and I remembered seeing the movie *Cleopatra* for the first time when I was young. I fell in love with her then.

The romantic scenes with Richard Burton were a little too steamy for my father's comfort—my sister and I weren't allowed to watch the entire movie. We had to wait for the rerun to finally see it all, by the time I was about fourteen. I watched it with my mother, who absolutely fell in love with Richard Burton. From then on, every time a new movie starring the two of them came out, my mother and I were the first ones in front of the television.

Other times, my thoughts drifted to Elizabeth as Cleopatra. She must have had a marvelous time playing the part of the Queen of Egypt. She was so beautiful, standing tall and proud with her on-scene son by her side. I remember that scene so vividly. The black kohl makeup around her eyes made her look even more powerful—it was captivating. I later learned that the kohl was not only for beauty but also used to ward off evil spirits and protect from the ever-present desert flies.

By late afternoon, we were entering the Nile River Lock—a man-made structure designed to raise or lower boats to match the river's changing water levels. It was fascinating to watch how our Dahabiya slipped into the narrow chamber, facing a tall, solid metal gate. Once we were fully inside, the rear gate closed behind us, and we were held in place as the chamber slowly filled with water.

The space was just wide enough to accommodate our boat, and we could feel the gentle shift as the water level rose. We waited as the chamber filled, lifting us until we reached the height of the river ahead. Then, the front gates slowly opened, retreating into the sides, and just like that, we were on our way to the grand city of Luxor.

THE CITY OF LUXOR

Our first stop across the Nile River from the Luxor area was a quick visit to the funerary temples of the Colossi of Memnon, which have long disappeared into the wind, but we were there to see the remaining two statues. It was a short bus ride from the boat. As we got off, three young girls stood anxiously waiting. They came right up to us, raising their hands to show us little handmade dolls they had sewn. One of the older girls kept encouraging the younger one to approach me, gently nudging her forward.

I could see the little doll, stitched by her unpracticed hands, as I tried to find some change in my pocket. Just as I handed her the coins, I saw a fly land in the corner of her eye, take a drink from her tear, and fly off. I couldn't believe what I had just seen—a thirsty fly had found an oasis. She didn't flinch; she just insisted I keep the doll.

I kept my sunglasses on for the rest of the trip, thinking about Cleopatra and her black kohl makeup to keep the flies away.

Our group followed our excellent guide, Omar, down the path for a closer look at the two giant statues of Pharaoh Amenhotep III, known as Amenhotep the Magnificent and the grandfather of Tutankhamun. Amenhotep III ruled Egypt between 1386 and 1349 BC during a period of great prosperity and splendor. The seated statues stand at the entrance to what was once his grand mortuary temple, now long gone, leaving behind an open and spacious field.

Across the road, next to a dusty stretch of pavement, stood a row of humble shops selling souvenirs, refreshments, and snacks. I met a young father sitting in front of one with his son. We exchanged smiles and a few words, though neither of us understood the other. In the distant mountains, I could see a sandy little town, likely home to the young girls and shopkeepers we'd just met.

Our next stop was the Valley of the Kings. Again, it was a short ride on the bus, right up to the sandy, rocky, beige mountains. Off the bus and walking again—with the sun beaming down through my white gauze scarf—I found it very difficult to appreciate certain moments. Usually, it was when I had to walk from the bus to the temple door, and I was excited to enter. I often trailed behind.

Sofia sometimes chose not to stray far from the bus. She never really shared much about her previous trip to Egypt, but I gathered she had been on this tour before. I finally reached one of the entrances where Santiago was waiting for me. I noticed he sometimes watched out for me when I lagged, especially when the heat slowed me down. The security guards were there for our safety, but not to carry me.

As I joined Santiago, we walked into the first chamber, and we were utterly amazed by how well-preserved the tomb of Ramesses VI was (KV9—Valley of the Kings, location #9). The hieroglyphic paintings in some areas of the walls were so vivid in color. In particular, the cobalt—Egyptian Blue—stood out. It was the same powdered pigment shaped into small pyramids among the spice and herb stalls at the bazaar in Cairo. Such rich, brilliant blues and earthy browns made from copper; it was hard to believe these hues had survived so many centuries.

Omar wasn't with Santiago and me to describe some of the scenes. Still, the paintings reflected rituals and offerings to the gods, etched in reverence to ensure safe passage into eternal life. I had once heard that

Egyptian men expected seven maidens to wait on them in the afterlife. I looked for that story in the paintings, hoping to find it, but I never did. It must be there somewhere.

As we moved into the descending chambers, we examined the walls displaying funerary scenes from the *Litany of Ra*, the sun god. We then entered Rames's burial chamber, where the broken red granite sarcophagus lay in the center beneath a stunning ceiling painted with astronomical scenes of the goddess Nut.

Her story is fascinating. It was one I may have heard before, but certainly didn't remember. Seeing it in person, I knew I'd remember it forever. In the painting, Nut swallows Ra each night and gives birth to him, the sun, each morning. It was precisely as Omar had described in his briefing before we got off the bus.

We looked closely at the details and were careful not to touch anything as we moved around the chamber on a raised wooden walkway, designed to protect the site from the wear of countless tourists' feet. Surprisingly, the temperature inside was cool and tolerable—a natural climate that helps preserve the colors and carvings.

Santiago pulled out his camera since we were the last tourists heading out of one of the chambers.

I looked at him in disbelief. "You're not allowed to take pictures inside the tombs," I whispered.

He glanced at me with a sly smile and a crooked wink.

"No te preocupes."

"What?! *Don't worry?* I don't want to end up in jail for a thousand years!" I hissed as I walked off, distancing myself from the offender.

It was only a few discreet pictures, but Omar's words started playing in my head. He had told us stories passed down from Mr. Hawass, the famous Egyptian archaeologist, about treasures taken from tombs that carried bad omens. A few years later, I'd hear about a woman somewhere in the States who had been plagued by a streak of misfortune. She eventually contacted Mr. Hawass to return the artifacts she had in her home. She had heard him speak publicly about the so-called curses some antiquities carried. I even saw him on television around that time, discussing the success of his campaign to recover stolen treasures. Several had been returned—some, apparently, out of fear.

Santiago only had time to take a few pictures, but we are supposed to follow the directives: no touching, no photos inside the tombs, and don't even think of taking anything . . . or risk being cursed!

Stepping out into the bright sunlight, I was disappointed to learn that the tomb of Tutankhamun—discovered in 1922 with over 5,000 artifacts— was currently closed to tourists for restoration. The tomb was now bare, with everything cataloged and stored away for safekeeping. The beautiful golden casket, the famous burial headpiece, and several other artifacts were displayed at the Egyptian Museum in Cairo.

Thankfully, I would have a few extra days in Cairo after the cruise to rehearse and perform—just enough time to visit the museum and see those treasures in person.

LUXOR TEMPLE

The magnificent Luxor Temple is the next temple dedicated to the god Amun-Ra—a merged deity of Amun, the mysterious creator of Thebes (now known as Luxor), and Ra, the sun god. Amun-Ra was one of the most powerful figures in ancient Egyptian religion. The temple is connected by the grand Avenue of Sphinxes, a ceremonial path stretching a mile and three-quarters. Before reaching the temple entrance, you're welcomed by the 650 surviving sphinxes and ram-headed statues with lion bodies, perfectly aligned on either side of the avenue.

As you approach the towering seventy-nine-foot entrance wall, made from mudbrick and sandstone, you're greeted by two gigantic twenty-foot seated statues of Ramesses II, flanking a seventy-five-foot obelisk that stands proudly at the gateway.

Some nights, when the temple is open, the lights offer a dramatic presentation—something I saw in videos, but unfortunately, I wasn't there at night. In fact, by the time we arrived, after a long ride from the side street bus parking lot, I was so hot that I was relieved we didn't have to walk through the Avenue of Sphinxes. To my right, I could see the avenue stretching on forever.

Just before arriving at the temple's entrance, we noticed a large crowd of tourists, about twenty-five people. Sofia and I walked closer and heard voices echoing in the sandy yard. As we stepped in, we saw what was going on: people were gathered around a man on the ground. A strong-looking woman was trying to get him to fold his knees and shouting something at him as he resisted.

By her language, it seemed she was German, and it was clear that they didn't understand each other. She was on her knees, leaning over the old man, and as I got closer, I heard him calling out:

"Aléjate, muévete, déjame en paz, estoy bien, suéltame."

I stepped forward and told the woman, "Get off of him, he's saying to get off him."

"It's okay, I'm a nurse," she replied, trying to reassure me.

"But he says he's fine and to get off him. Let him breathe! Get off!" I insisted.

Reluctantly, the nurse got off him, muttering that she was a nurse and knew what she was doing. She joined her group just as the paramedics arrived with a stretcher.

As the crowd began to disperse, I started talking with the Spanish gentleman. He explained that he had been feeling too hot and had fainted, but he insisted that all he needed was water to cool off.

When he saw the stretcher, he begged, "Diles que no me lleven al hospital. Yo no voy para que me cobran. Estoy bien."

I tried to explain that the paramedics were determined to take him away, but he begged again.

"Diles que me dejen en paz, estoy bien. Yo no voy para que me cobran. ¡Estoy bien!"

He kept repeating that he was fine, that he didn't want to go to the hospital because they would charge him when he was perfectly fine. He was adamant.

I offered to accompany him to the hospital as an interpreter, since no one else spoke Spanish.

I told Sofia I was going with the gentleman and asked her to let Omar know I was getting in the ambulance. The paramedics were quick to strap him in, and the stretcher was rolled away with me running alongside, following them into the ambulance.

The old man continued to plead, "No quiero que me lleven al hospital. No voy a pagar. Diles que me dejen en paz."

He kept insisting that they shouldn't take him to the hospital. He didn't want to pay and demanded they drop him off at his hotel instead.

Finally, the driver asked for the hotel's name and agreed to drop us off. The old man was able to walk off the stretcher without any issue and made his way into the hotel, with me following behind. He turned to me and said, "Come in, let's order a drink."

I looked around outside and saw nothing but sand and very few houses.

It had a classic, old-style interior, reminiscent of something out of the movie *Casablanca*—but this was Egypt. The wooden reception desk, which was less than twelve feet long, was located on the left side. The whole room had low ceilings and a warm, red-toned feel. The carpet was a red floral design, with red velvet easy chairs and a couple of sofas featuring dark patterns. We sat in the easy chairs next to a red and beige striped curtained window to the right of the room.

The gentleman ordered us drinks and was very thankful that I had accompanied him to the hotel. He began to explain why he was in Egypt alone. He told me he had visited years before on his honeymoon and wanted to return to relive those memories after his wife had passed away. He said his children had tried to dissuade him from coming, fearing something might happen to him due to his age. That's why he had been so adamant about not wanting to go to the hospital—he didn't want them to find out and make him stop traveling altogether.

As he continued sharing the beautiful story of his wife, I noticed Omar walked into the hotel and went straight to the front desk. I waved to him, and he quickly walked over to join us.

"You should never have left the group," Omar said as he approached.

"But no one spoke Spanish, and he didn't want to go to the hospital," I explained.

"Let's go," Omar insisted.

"But we ordered a drink," I said.

"We must leave now. Everyone is waiting on the bus outside," he pleaded as he looked at me urgently.

I thought, *Well, no drink and this is the end of this adventure. This was starting off to be the most thrilling part of the day so far.*

I never remembered the old man's name or the quirky hotel, but it was—like the old man suggested—a place to return to and refresh a memory that felt like a dream.

SHARM EL-SHEIKH

The next morning, we were up early to catch a flight to the resort town of Sharm el-Sheikh. It's located at the southern tip of Mount Sinai, where the land dips into the Egyptian blue of the Red Sea. Really, it was the reflection of the clear blue sky, as I saw it from the window during the short flight. Shortly after, I was looking out the bus window as we traveled through the town toward our hotel.

There wasn't much to see. Sandy, jagged mountains formed the backdrop. Along the main road were a few shops and some small hotels, two or three stories tall at most. I thought, perhaps because of the heat—or maybe for other reasons—not many floors of rooms were needed in such a hot place.

The heat remained on my mind, as my forehead was always moist. I figured maybe I'd lose some of the weight I gained from eating so many pastries that were always waiting in my cabin.

A beeping sound caught my attention. There was light traffic up ahead, and the sound of a bulldozer backing up echoed through the bus. I looked out and saw a hotel being torn down. As we drove past, Omar explained it was a hotel that had been bombed months earlier.

That's when it hit me—the importance of writing articles about the beauty of Egypt. We were here to help promote tourism in Sharm el-Sheikh, which had suffered since the 2004 bombing. And now, in 2005, it was right in front of me as I watched the demolition.

When we arrived at the hotel, we were greeted by the director, a tall, jolly German man who welcomed us with cool refreshments in the lobby. He was there to answer any questions and share what was available to us during our stay.

The beach was one option: we could snorkel in the clear blue water and spot the many colorful fish that live just below the surface. Another option was scuba diving with the area sharks. I knew I wasn't going out there, but our photojournalist and Santiago took up the offer without hesitation.

The third option was to stay at the resort and enjoy everything it had to offer, including the gym and the swimming pools. We had the same options on day two—or we could visit Saint Catherine's Monastery. Omar shared that it was a Greek Orthodox monastery located near the place where Moses was said to have descended from Mount Sinai, where the stone tablets were inscribed with the Ten Commandments.

Everyone except the photojournalist chose the monastery. Sofia opted out, too—she stayed behind to make her calls, still trying to confirm her appointment with Dr. Hawass once we returned to Cairo.

We all checked into our rooms, and once again, I was greeted by a basket full of mini, sweet Danish pastries and other delicious treats, along with a generous arrangement of fresh fruit. There were even flowers in the room.

It was a cozy space with an arched alcove painted in colorful Arabic designs. The alcove formed a charming sitting area where I lay back and nibbled on pastries. I admired the brass lamps with their colorful glass shades and matching brass tables as I ate. Even the bathroom fixtures had elegant brass accents.

It felt like stepping onto another movie set. The only thing missing for me was a bottle of champagne.

After stuffing myself, I dressed for the beach—it would be my only chance to swim in the Red Sea. I stepped outside, heading toward the beach, and it felt like walking under a burning furnace. The sun blazed down on my unprotected scalp, almost as if it were sitting directly on top of me.

The hotel grounds stretched far, with many townhouse-style rooms lining the path. It was nearly two blocks before I finally reached the water. As soon as I stepped in, I swear steam must have risen off my body.

I slipped on my snorkeling mask and waded in—only about three feet—and I could already see the little colorful tropical fish darting below. There were so many. I saw yellow fish with black masks over their eyes that instantly made me think of Cleopatra. Then came the parrotfish, nibbling at the coral, and even the little clownfish, playfully darting in and out of their hiding spots.

I hadn't known that the Red Sea was considered one of the world's best diving and snorkeling spots, but it certainly earned that title. I just wish I had a partner to share such an incredible experience with. No matter how hot it was, this moment was unforgettable.

SAINT CATHERINE'S MONASTERY

We left on our journey just after our early breakfast, carrying our picnic basket, which the hotel had prepared. We were all ready to go on the journey up Mount Sinai. The monastery was not open to tourists at that time but would allow our group since it was a government-sponsored tour with security.

As I stepped onto the bus, I noticed an additional security man, and that the guards now carried automatic rifles. Omar filled us in, saying that on occasion, there have been incidents of ambushes from local smugglers and bandits. With the bombing in Sharm el-Sheikh, which resulted in eighty-eight fatalities, the Egyptian government was always on alert for small groups of terrorists. With so many mountains, I could see how easily any group could hide behind the granite and sandstone formations.

I doubt that anyone in our group knew the full details of the fatalities. I had heard about the bombing, but it was not something I remembered when Egypt was first mentioned to me. I'm sure the excitement at the opportunity blocked out any negative facts about traveling there.

If I had remembered the details of the bombing, I probably would have said no thanks to the trip.

For the first hour, we saw jagged mountains of granite in all shades of sandstone before arriving at our first Bedouin rest stop, which gave us a chance to stretch our legs and purchase any souvenirs. The Bedouin people are a nomadic Arab group residing in the deserts, known for sharing water or shelter with guests as part of their traditional cultural practices. As Santiago and I looked around, there was only a basket with about four hand-carved canes, some rocks, and not much else. I was ready to buy something, but Santiago beat me to the better-looking cane, so I left some bills under a stone on the table. We stepped into the low, flat-roofed blanket tent, which was made of wind-worn blankets crafted from camel or goat hair. We could have sat on the cushions around the room as the nomad invited us with a show of hands, but we decided to return to the bus since we were the last ones.

Our next stop was the Israel-Egypt Peace Treaty Monument commemorating the signing of the treaty in 1979. As a fan of President Carter, I had always understood that he brokered the treaty in 1979, and I was proud of his role in such a critical moment. However, when I saw the monument, it was President Clinton who was featured. Perhaps his involvement in peace talks during the 1990s played a part in that, but I couldn't help feeling a bit confused.

The security men showed real pride as they talked among themselves in cheerful-sounding voices, as it was their first time traveling to Saint Catherine's. It was also the final security checkpoint. We all got out to take pictures.

Omar shouted out, "Okay, next stop in about ten minutes is the monastery."

We arrived at the monastery's thick sandstone fortress walls. With the great mountains behind it, it appeared as a secluded, sacred fortress. All along the drive up, there was quietness as we gazed at the mountains, and when we arrived, we lowered our voices in respect for the holy grounds as we were let inside. A Greek monk led the way, sharing a few details in his quiet voice as we all listened with our necks stretched out to hear him. After a few minutes, he invited us to join him in prayer during the session, which was taking place in a chapel. We were allowed to sit quietly and listen to the voices in worship by the dozen or so monks sitting in booths and chairs lining two of the walls. The aroma of frankincense filled the room, and the voices of prayer echoed from the ceiling and down into the dark, wood-lined chapel.

The monastery is named after Saint Catherine of Alexandria, a fourth-century Christian martyr. Known for her wisdom, eloquence, and her strong Christian faith, she was executed for converting pagan philosophers and soldiers to Christianity. The miracle believed is that angels transported her body to where the monastery was then built in her honor. But it also protects the burning bush, said to be where God spoke to Moses. After the Vatican, Saint Catherine's is also known to have one of the oldest collections of Christian manuscripts and icons.

While we were sitting in the chapel, Santiago quietly stood up and left. I had already said my prayers, thanking the Lord for my safety on this trip, and quietly followed him out. We began walking around the chapel and onto a path that led us around the fortress, which felt more like a small neighborhood. At one point, we saw a group of women in their abayas and hijabs coming from a downstairs chamber. We assumed they were the women who helped maintain the premises. I wanted to make contact and simply say hello, but they turned the corner ahead of us and seemed to disappear.

The monastery was built to provide Christian monks with both a spiritual and physical sanctuary. A preserved handprint of Prophet Muhammad is said to exist at the monastery, which is believed to offer protection. It also protected Greek Orthodox monks who traveled here on pilgrimages to Mount Sinai, making it a historically significant religious site. Today, a few Greek Orthodox monks continue to maintain the monastery, caring for and protecting this revered ground.

We continued walking along the path until we reached the water well and the great burning bush. There it was. It appeared as though it was always watered by water seeping out from the well. This was truly a highlight of the trip, as I had heard and even seen the burning bush in the Moses movies, especially the one with Charlton Heston. I had always assumed this was the same well where, in the film, Moses meets his wife, with the burning bush framing their encounter. But I recalled Omar saying that Moses was from another town. I realized this wasn't the same well. Actually, Moses met his wife, Zipporah, at a well in a nearby town. But it is said that this is where Moses heard God's voice to go to the mountain.

I stepped outside the compound to use the tourist bathroom, and when I returned to the monastery's entrance, Santiago was talking to one of the monks. He approached me and asked if I would take a picture of them. It turned out the monk was from Argentina and was thrilled to speak with Santiago, a fellow countryman. I then asked if I could take a picture, and the monk initially seemed to agree. But just two seconds later, he apologized, saying that he really couldn't. It was against his religion to even speak with a woman. He quietly said goodbye to Santiago and waved goodbye to me.

We headed back to the hotel in Sharm el-Sheikh for a shower, dinner, and a late flight back to Cairo. When we arrived, Sofia was waiting for us in the lobby. Omar shared that he had received notice that our appointment with Dr. Zahi Hawass was confirmed. Sofia immediately got upset.

"The appointment was for me only, not for the whole group," she said, her voice rising.

Omar replied calmly, "No, we all go as a group. The appointment is at 10:00 a.m.; right after that, we'll head straight to the airport for your return to New York City. Adela, you'll join us as well, but after the appointment, a driver will take you to the Cultural Wheel to meet everyone."

Sofia stormed off, and we didn't see her again until we were all on the bus headed to the airport. She sat down beside me and expressed how upset she was that she wasn't getting her solo visit. It was the main reason she had joined the tour. I felt bad for her, but thought something was better than nothing. At least she'd have the chance to meet him face-to-face, and maybe she could try to make another arrangement.

BACK IN CAIRO

The next morning, we walked into Dr. Hawass's office. What a lively, friendly man! He greeted us all with a smile, shaking our hands and quickly telling us about the expedition he was currently working on. We took turns snapping pictures with each other's cameras, which got a little confusing. As we said our goodbyes and expressed our thanks, I noticed Sofia linger behind, finally having her moment to talk with Dr. Hawass alone. *Good for her*, I thought. I'd be upset too if I had to sit under the hot sun for days without getting my own appointment. Whatever it was she wanted to say to him in person, I was glad she had the chance.

We stepped outside, exchanged our goodbyes, and then the bus pulled away as my car arrived to take me to the cultural center.

EGYPTIAN MUSEUM

I was dropped off and informed that I had the day off. No one was available at the cultural center, and they'd meet me tomorrow at the rehearsal. The driver would return the following day to take me, but the time had not been confirmed yet. He handed me a sheet with information and said he'd call once the schedule was set. I glanced at the papers: one was a city map, the other had information on how to use the metro. I was happy to have a day to myself, though I only had time to either visit the museum or make the long trip to Alexandria. I really wanted to see the Mediterranean Sea and visit the Bibliotheca Alexandrina, but I wouldn't have time for both, and I didn't want to return too late. So, I decided to stay closer to the city.

I changed into comfortable clothes and set off on my adventure in Cairo. I followed the map toward the metro but made a quick stop to buy a bottle of water. The shopkeeper chuckled as I handed him a dollar for the water, which I knew was more than enough. Within a few blocks, I reached the subway and was pleasantly surprised by how clean it was—there were only a couple of advertising posters on the cement walls and a quiet, calm atmosphere. I also noticed there wasn't a ticket booth. There were a few ticket machines, but I couldn't read the language. No one was around. I waited, thinking, *Surely someone will show up.*

I then heard footsteps coming down the stairs—leather sandals slapping against the concrete. A tall, handsome young man with a soft, white *cheche* scarf wrapped around his neck and striking greenish eyes appeared. I asked him for help with buying a ticket. He was very kind.

"You only need ten cents, but Egyptian money," he said as he reached into his canvas shoulder bag, slipped the coins into the machine, and let me through the gate, followed by himself.

"Thanks, that's so kind of you! Let me pay you back," I said.

He smiled and waved it off. "Please, don't worry. It's only ten cents. Everything is affordable here," he said as we passed through the gate.

"You speak English so well," I commented.

"Yes, I try. I'm a student here at the university. It's much cheaper than Algeria, but I went to America when I was young and learned to speak," he explained as we got on the train.

"Where are you going?" he asked.

"To see the mummies in the museum," I replied.

He chuckled lightly. "Oh, there are a lot of mummies, even cat mummies! It's three more stops for you. I get off at the next stop. When you get thirsty, try the cool water from the *zeer (a clay water vessel)* they have in the square. Nice to meet you," he said, waving goodbye as he got off the train.

I thought about how nice he had been and what a wonderful experience I was having, though I still felt a little lonely and wished I weren't alone. I recalled the many amazing trips I had taken and daydreamed that one day, I would have a new partner by my side—to hold me, kiss me, keep me close—and, well . . . maybe to help me carry my luggage sometimes.

The train stopped. "My stop," I muttered to myself, and off I went.

When I stepped out, I found myself in front of the Museum of Egyptian Antiquities, also known as the Tahrir Museum, because of its location in the historic Tahrir Square (Liberation Square). Since the mid-1800s, its long history has seen revolutions, demonstrations, and expressions through art, murals, and even protest graffiti.

The aging museum, designed by French architect Marcel Dourgnon, opened in 1902. Situated at the edge of Tahrir Square, it takes full advantage of the open space, allowing the salmon-colored building to shine. Mexican palms were planted around the museum, selected for their rapid growth, which would tower over the Egyptian statues that guard the treasures inside. The grand façade entrance is reminiscent of a Roman triumphal arch, like the Arc de Triomphe.

As I walked in, I was greeted by towering statues of kings, queens, and deities. There were mummies—some old, some fresh—still unpacked from the visible crates. In the various rooms, tall black glass cases displayed mummified cats, while others had no glass. Some mummies were so close you could almost breathe right on top of them. Of course, I didn't dare—I was fearful of inhaling a spirit.

The museum felt dusty, likely from the comings and goings of new excavations. As I walked from room to room, it seemed like the space was bursting at the seams. There were too many amazing artifacts and treasures to take in.

There was little security until I reached King Tut's chamber. You needed a special ticket to enter the air-controlled, dimly lit room. Inside, the displays were carefully illuminated, showcasing the most famous treasures.

Tutankhamun became king at a young age and ruled until he was eighteen or nineteen years old. His name means "Living Image of Amun," who was one of the most powerful gods of ancient Egypt. He is famous mainly because of the discovery of his tomb in 1922 in the Valley of the Kings, which contained over 5,000 pieces of ancient treasure.

I stepped into the small room and was immediately confronted by the golden inner casket, a breathtaking piece with intricate details. Seeing it in person was a rare treasure in itself. Countless documentaries and films showcase it, but nothing compares to seeing it up close. The casket is adorned with the youthful face of King Tut, who is wearing the striped royal headdress we've all seen in movies. On his forehead, a vulture and cobra symbolize his rule over Upper and Lower Egypt. The rest of the headpiece is decorated with small tubular glass beads, lapis lazuli, and turquoise. The casket itself is inlaid with hieroglyphics, containing prayers and protective spells from the *Book of the Dead* to guide him into the afterlife.

The rest of the room held display cases filled with personal items—rings, bracelets, necklaces—and even a pair of golden shoes for the afterlife. I was overwhelmed by the sheer number of treasures, and I couldn't help but think about Egypt's wealth. Despite being a country often considered poor; its ancient riches are staggering. I hoped the country would remain safe and tourists would continue to visit. Egypt is truly remarkably wealthy in ancient treasures and history.

Once bursting at the seams, the museum has now divided its treasures between the original Museum of Egyptian Antiquities in Tahrir Square and the new Grand Egyptian Museum in Giza, near the Pyramids.

EL SAWY CULTURAL WHEEL

I was so overwhelmed that I didn't even remember how I got back to my room. After the airport arrival, the appointment with Dr. Hawass, and the visit to the museum, exhaustion hit me hard. I didn't wake up until the phone rang the next day. The driver was there to take me to the rehearsal and then dinner.

The cultural center is a vibrant hub for entertainment and the arts. Inside, a large stage with air conditioning hosts musical performances, while outside, smaller stages and creative areas are set up for various forms of artistic expression. It's a great hangout for young people. Egypt lacks much space, so the directors and members are grateful for the center's existence. I, too, was thankful for the opportunity to visit and perform in such a culturally rich place.

The next day, the concert went smoothly. The Russian pianist and the rest of the band were fantastic, and there were no issues with the music. They were a warm, intuitive group, making the experience even more enjoyable.

As I stepped onto the stage, the audience welcomed me under the soft glow of the lights, with Cairo's pulse humming in the background. It was a beautiful exchange of culture, rhythm, and heart.

After the concert, a group of us walked outside, and the sound of loud singing reached my ears. Drawn to the sound, I approached and saw a group of about twenty young people singing joyfully in unison. I wish I knew the language so that I could join the fun.

By morning, I was on my flight home thinking, *What a hot place, but what an absolutely wonderful experience.*

I finally woke up in my own bed, without rocking in the waves, smoky odors, or melodious beeping car horns. *Did I just wake up from a dream?* I wondered.

To stay safe while traveling, register at mytravel.state.gov to register for the Smart Traveler Enrollment Program (STEP), a free service to receive emergency information while traveling.

CHAPTER 8

MujeresLatinas.com

By the mid-nineties, the internet was quickly gaining ground. My brother encouraged me to buy a computer and start a website, predicting that the internet would become the tool of the future, here to stay forever. At first, I didn't believe him, but soon, I saw how quickly my friends were discussing how easy it would be to create promotional flyers, send messages, and build mailing lists.

Before that, we used stencils and a lot of tape to create flyers, which we mailed using postage stamps. Mailing lists were typed, printed on sticky labels, and carefully added to envelopes—it was so time-consuming, I can hardly believe we managed it! We even printed poster-size flyers and stapled them to wooden barricades surrounding NYC construction sites, covering them with layers of advertisements, giving the streets a sense of vibrant, dynamic energy—colorful and alive, yet sometimes chaotic and cluttered.

We also learned how the Mac computer would become key to making music in the future. My son, Miles, was already using his Atari computer to make beats in the late eighties and later switched to a Mac to use music programs like Logic and Pro Tools. In the early days, these programs involved a lot of manual reading and self-study, but I didn't have the time or interest to delve into them. Instead, I found myself drawn to mentoring.

I had read an article in a major newspaper about the high dropout rates in Latino communities, and it made me feel embarrassed. My boys were in school, and I had them on track. I was grateful that we lived in New York City, in the right neighborhood—one filled with diverse schools, STEM programs, art institutions, museums, and cultural centers. These resources were available for those who sought them out or were introduced by motivating teachers. Living in a big city, where parents actively searched for the best schools they could afford, put me in a position to find opportunities. Teachers were encouraging their students to excel, as their success reflected not only their own efforts but also the quality of their teaching. It was a stark contrast to my own school experience, where teachers were often more interested in the bell ringing to send us home. Quality teachers were few and far between in my steel mill community when I was growing up. I used to tell my sister that we were being groomed to be the wives of the male graduates who would follow their fathers into the mill.

Never having had a daughter to guide, I felt a strong need to offer something inspirational to the girls who didn't have role models or mentors, just as I hadn't when I was in high school. No one I knew had gone to college, and with no one talking about it, it wasn't on my mind to inquire about it. Many Latina women from my generation, especially those from blue-collar families, only had a high school education or less. My parents had both stopped school after the fifth grade to work.

I did have a science teacher in eleventh grade who motivated me to engage more with my classes. He even took me to visit a research lab at the local hospital. However, my dad then moved us from Gary to East Chicago, and I lost touch with my only mentor. By the time I started my senior year at my new high school, I was anxious to graduate and leave town. I had already had a taste of life in a big city like Chicago, having stayed with cousins during summer weekends and started my new job while completing my final two classes.

Every decade or so, I would question my future and my knowledge, which was mostly limited to music and cultural exchanges from the places I had visited and the people I had met. I hadn't yet made up my mind about earning a college degree. I was working steadily as a singer and doing side jobs to ensure my boys were financially supported through college. For me, there was never a question about them not going.

My son Billy, the oldest, was all about his education. So much so that after completing the required semester of music at my request, he declared that academics were more important. Good for him—he went on to become a state legislator at the young age of twenty-six, then earned his law degree, and is now also a successful entrepreneur.

Miles, on the other hand, didn't have an explicit declaration, so I made the decision for him to continue with piano lessons. But his heart was really in music production, so I bought him an Apple computer to help him continue learning. Eventually, he began earning a living by adding music to commercials, movies, producing work for singers, and playing piano at various events.

Once I saw that the boys were on their way to running their own lives, I began thinking again about starting college. In the meantime, I was invited to perform in Washington, D.C., for the first symposium of Latinas in Business in 1997. I was excited to perform for a large audience of women, but I thought, *What will I sing to them? They won't be coming with their husbands or partners. They'll be coming with their co-workers.* I decided I needed a motivational closing song—something empowering.

I mentioned it to a DJ friend, who offered to search for some suggestions. When I listened to the cassette tape he compiled for me, I didn't hear anything that truly conveyed the message I wanted to share. I had a great band to back me, and finally, a week before the symposium, a simple phrase came to me as the hook of the song.

Somos Mujeres Latinas

Somos mujeres. Somos Latinas.
Somos mujeres unidas. mujeres Latinas.
(We are women. We are Latinas. We are
united women. Latina women.)

We were at the venue, performing the final song, when I saw the women rise to their feet. Dina, who had come along with me and the band, led them to the front of the stage, raising their fists in the air and rocking their hips to the beat. Some of the women sang along to the hook of the song, reading from the palm cards Dina had distributed during soundcheck. We had typed up the lyrics, printed a hundred cards, and added my contact information—essentially an oversized business card. When they heard their country mentioned in the salute, they cheered loudly. It was an electrifying moment. The song was a hit. The women seemed to stand a little taller, visibly proud and empowered.

The director of the symposium came straight over, saying, "What a great song as the closing anthem!"

She added that she would love to have the song for the next event. When she called it an "anthem," I thought, *Yes! I wrote an anthem! Wow, this is amazing. Now, what can I do with this song?*

Excited by the song's success, I couldn't wait to get home. I now had a reason to start the website. I had a song to promote and an idea for creating a platform to highlight the profiles of inspiring Latinas and providing mentorship for young women in search of role models.

Sitting down at my computer, I typed "MujeresLatinas.com" into the domain search bar. It was available. Of course, it was for sale, but it was very affordable through a web hosting and domain registrar at the time. I hesitated before clicking send. *How much would it cost me monthly?* I didn't need another expense. I stopped myself, thinking, *Let me not act in haste. I'll think on it for a day.* Meanwhile, people were snatching up URLs, regardless of whether they had plans for the site. Resellers were grabbing names to sell or auction off.

The next day, I was busy with rehearsal for a gig later that weekend. I had errands to run—dry cleaning, buying nylons, getting my nails done, and shopping for food. The weekend arrived, and after Saturday's gig, it was finally Sunday. I decided that *today, I'll buy the URL.*

I typed the name in again, thinking, *who wouldn't want to grab MujeresLatinas.com with the hundreds of millions of Latinas worldwide it represented?*

I typed it in . . . and "Oh no!" The sign that popped up said, "Under Construction." The name was taken. I had waited too long. I muttered, "Damn, I lost my name. Someone beat me to it."

Reflecting, I realized that I have a bad habit of hesitating when it comes to spending money. It's like I fear success or wasting money. I tend to delay decisions. Sometimes it works out, and I save money on things I don't need. But lately, I remind myself to act quickly and make decisions as soon as an idea occurs to me. Life moves fast, and someone else might grab it first. It's like a thought floating in the air, waiting for someone to reach up and snatch it.

I mentioned to my brother that I had lost the name. "Of course," he said, "I told you to move on it!"

I shrugged, thinking, *Oh, well, I'll come up with another name that works.*

At the marketing department of Bear Stearns, where I was working at the time, everyone was talking about a similar issue with the company's domain name. Since I was part of the marketing team, I was privy to the details. Apparently, they had been ready to register the company's domain name when they discovered that flippers had scooped it up. The names were listed in various combinations: BearStearns.com, BS.com, Bear.com. And the worst part? The site featured photos of bear-chested men—definitely not the right image for an investment bank. When the company reached out, the owner demanded thousands of dollars to transfer the name. Management didn't want to pay, so they got lawyers involved and ended up using trademark laws to reclaim the name.

The following week, I checked MujeresLatinas.com again—still under construction. Time passed, and I forgot about it for a while. But when I checked again a few weeks later, I was shocked. My jaw dropped. I called my brother over to take a look. He looked at it and started laughing. I was insulted. The website was an adult site. I thought, *Oh my... these poor, lost souls.*

I was even more determined to find a way to empower young women. I was angry. I thought about the people who built such a site. Shutting down my computer, I muttered, "I hope they waste their money on that trash." I didn't even know if it was a man or a woman behind it.

I kept brainstorming new names for the site, weighing the cost of building and maintaining a website. Meanwhile, I checked in periodically to see if MujeresLatinas.com was still up. Five months later, I checked again—and surprise—the site was gone. I wondered what had happened. The most likely explanation? They hadn't figured out how to monetize it. The technology wasn't in place, or maybe they couldn't handle the cost.

I quickly looked up the owner in the registry and found an email address. I decided to send a brief message:

Dear Owner of MujeresLatinas.com

I noticed you have taken your site down. I would like to ask, if you are not using the name would you please consider transferring the name to us. We are a group of women who want to build the site to include profiles on notable Latinas to help young women find role models and mentors.

Thank you kindly,

Adela Dalto

I thought, *Well, let's see what happens.* I wondered if he'd ask me to buy it from him, and if I would be willing to pay more than the standard fee that domain registrars charge. I kept thinking about it as I waited to hear back, assuming it was a guy I was writing to.

The very next day, I checked my email and was surprised to find a response. I started reading:

Dear Ladies,

Under the circumstances, I would very much like to give you the name for your mission. Here is the information you need to switch the ownership, and good luck.

I couldn't believe it. The person just handed over the name to me—no money, no request for credit. He seemed genuinely compassionate about the cause—or maybe he just didn't think to sell it to me. Who knows? But I was beyond thrilled. I got my name back—a name that fit perfectly with my song and now my website.

With that victory, my next step was clear: I would start an all-female band to perform empowerment songs, encouraging women to seek out role models and mentors who could help guide them toward a successful, fulfilling life.

Okay, now I had a plan. It was time to move forward.

*Do you have an idea you're passionate about? Don't wait
too long to act on it, and don't give up trying.*

CHAPTER 9

The Show Must Go On

As soon as I could, I began seeking help to build my website. I already had one for my singing career, but this new site would focus on Latina profiles, the anthem, and other valuable resources about Latina culture. At the time, I was working in a marketing department with a team of experts in graphic design, web development, and internet technology. They were willing to help me, as website building was my latest endeavor, and my coworkers generously shared their time and expertise. Within a few weeks, *MujeresLatinas.com* was born.

Next, I began putting together an all-female band to perform the anthem. We played in parades along 5th Avenue in Manhattan and at various women's events. It was exciting and a lot of fun. There's something exhilarating about singing to proud Latinas, watching them express their culture through dancing and singing along, and waving their hands in the air when they hear their country mentioned. We saluted all nineteen Spanish-speaking Latin American countries and Brazil, which speaks Portuguese.

My work and career were moving along like a bouncing ball on the lines of a musical staff filled with joyful music. By this point, I had already recorded three CDs and traveled to places like Venezuela, Singapore, and Bali. I was productive, singing with my Latin jazz band, and simultaneously moving forward with projects like the website. I also had the girl band, and a CD of empowerment music with the ladies that could propel the *Mujeres Latinas* band even further.

The only thing that wasn't going well was a relationship I had at the time. After a few years, I could feel something wasn't right, but I kept ignoring the signs. By this point, I was overwhelmed organizing a big concert, which had been his idea to begin with. He wasn't a musician, but he knew how to create a production schedule. He helped plan the event, working out the details for the timeline and breaking down the budget, which he presented to me in a bright blue binder. I had to secure a conductor, new musical arrangements (which included a string section, horns, and Latin percussion), and three special guests. The concert would feature forty-four musicians and four arrangers for the new material, including romantic Latin standards and mambos. I also needed two stage gowns—and, of course, comfortable shoes.

There were new songs with lyrics I had to memorize while searching for a producer or venue to buy the production. After approaching a couple of concert promoters, they told me I was being too ambitious. They said the budget for such a concert would be too high. A non-classical concert of Latin and Latin jazz music using strings had never been produced in New York City. I would be the first person to present a grand Latin music concert with strings. Latin music had always been presented with a big band or a Salsa band, typically for dancing. Additionally, I believe the promoters thought I didn't have the star power to sell out a two-hour show.

While I continued my search for a venue or promoter, suddenly, the world stopped. It was a clear, sunny day, and I was about ten minutes late walking from the subway to my full-time job at Bear Stearns. When I stepped out of the elevator on the 57th floor of the annex office on 3rd Avenue and 55th Street, I was barely at the receptionist's desk when she shouted, "A plane just hit one of the Twin Towers!"

Someone from the main office had called to notify us. I quickly went downstairs to buy a radio, needing to know what was going on as the news unfolded. By the time I arrived at the store, only two radios remained. I paid and headed back to the office, walking down 3rd Avenue, when I noticed a plane flying relatively low, heading downtown. I walked faster, and by the time I got back, the receptionist said, "Another plane hit the towers."

I quickly handed her the radio, and the rest of the office gathered around. Eventually, a TV was set up in the conference room, and we all assembled. We were in shock, unable to believe our eyes. We saw fire pouring out of both buildings and people jumping from the towers. They looked like falling angels as I silently prayed for them and headed back to my desk.

It was terrifying to watch scenes on television that were impossible to erase from my mind. Not yet knowing what was truly happening, I listened to the radio for more details. I recalled a time when I was working in one of the towers, having an eerie feeling as I heard the expansion joints creak in the walls while looking in the bathroom mirror, brushing my hair. I calmly returned to my desk to retrieve my purse and jacket, then proceeded to walk all the way out of the building. I only returned several years later for a corporate event performance. I also remembered that my friend Mario Grillo, who ran an orchestra as the band leader, also worked as a chef at Windows on the World, but I didn't know if he was scheduled to work that day. I would have to wait to find out.

It was getting close to lunchtime, and the staff was getting restless, wondering why we weren't excused from the office. We looked out the windows and saw crowds of workers walking on the sidewalks below. We wondered if it was safer to stay inside or leave the building. Finally, at noon, we were allowed to leave. When we got downstairs, people were walking north from downtown, their hair and clothes covered in chalky white dust from the debris of the fallen towers. We joined the crowd, walking in silence.

All public transportation had stopped. The bridges and tunnels were closed, preventing travel to and from Manhattan. There was no reception for cell phones, making it impossible to reach loved ones. We could only try to get home and wait for communication from those who hadn't reported in as safe.

My brother was at the apartment when I arrived after the long walk home. He said he couldn't get home because the trains had been suspended, so he managed to get a cab. The landline phones were working, but it was a weekday, so most of our extended family was either at work, school, or somewhere trying to get home. My grandson's maternal grandmother called to ask what she should do about little Miles, who was at school downtown. She said she was home, making calls with her landline, but had been inside City Hall earlier when she felt a tremor under her feet. She was told to go home as the offices started to close, and people began to head out. She couldn't reach her daughter by cell phone due to the lack of service. Susan would be somewhere between her apartment in New Jersey and her train stop, which was located on the underground floors of the Twin Towers. It was her routine to take that route to her job in Manhattan. We were extremely worried because we were unable to reach her. Many people were stuck in the subway, having to walk out along the tracks to get out of the stations because all service had stopped. All we could do was wait for the cell phone service to be restored. Meanwhile, visions of falling souls would reappear in between my present thoughts of what families could be going through.

Spirits of The Lost

Spirits of the lost, can you hear me calling?
Spirits of the lost, can you hear me crying?
I have lost you from my sight,
I have lost you from my touch,
But I will never lose you from my heart.

Spirits of the lost, can you hear me singing?
Spirits of the lost, hear our voices ringing,
We have lost you from our reach,
Peace and love are what we'll preach,
And we will never, never lose you from our hearts.

Living on 89th Street on the West Side, I could now see the smoke from my window slowly drifting north towards us from the towers. After several hours of anxiety and uncertainty, the cell phone reception was finally restored, and the first call was from little Miles's mother. She was safe. She explained that by the time she reached the train station, the towers had already been hit, and the subway station was closed. She never got off the bus because it, too, wasn't going anywhere. People just sat on the bus waiting until she could return to her apartment by taking a yellow cab. We were all so relieved to hear from her. Everyone was now accounted for, and as the evening set, so did the sounds of the city. There was a stillness I had never felt before. The smoke had reached the Upper West Side, and a dark cloud of fear hung over the city as we waited to hear more about what was now identified as a terrorist attack. We tried to recall who else worked in the Twin Towers.

Meanwhile, I had a flash memory of the one time I returned to perform for a corporate event with my bass player friend Cucho Martinez. We had stood together in a corner of the salon where two gigantic glass windows met. We stood right up to the glass, imagining we were birds flying out at 106 floors high.

Many lives were changed as a result of this tragedy. Several months later, articles appeared in the papers about couples with solid relationships getting married, while those who didn't—like mine—started falling apart. I should have paid attention when he showed up one day at my door with roses that had no color. They weren't white; they were dull, like his feelings, but he didn't say anything about our relationship that day. I guess he couldn't find the words to clarify his intentions.

While trying to prevent a breakup, I kept pitching the project around and, finally, before the year was out, I found success. The concert would take place at Aaron Davis Hall, a venue at The City College of New York. It would be their highlight of the year, with a generous budget, billed as a Mother's Day concert. I felt so relieved and proud that they had accepted, but almost immediately, a new sense of urgency swept through me—the project would now move quickly with the date set.

I was ready to share the news with him at a lunch date he set up. Here I had great news, but instead, he started with the worst words I could hear: "I don't want this relationship anymore."

My heart sank to my feet. I thought it and then said it: "Oh no, not now, not when I have a production that you started, and now with a date for the concert."

What horrible timing. Couldn't he wait until after the concert? This was unnecessary stress while trying to organize so many details for the show. I was devastated by the breakup. I couldn't believe it was happening.

For the next few months, I continued to move forward. The program was already planned out, and arrangers were finishing the new musical charts. One of the arrangers would be the conductor, and I could now book musicians so they could reserve the date on their calendars. I was pushing ahead, although I was developing a nervous stomach. I had lost weight since the designer took the first measurements for the gowns, and with some adjustments, I couldn't believe how great I looked in the tight-fitting outfits. But just a couple of weeks before the concert, I couldn't keep anything in my stomach. Instead of feeling happy with the fantastic show ahead, I felt terrible from the breakup and feared I wouldn't have the energy to pull it off. The dresses had to be returned for further adjustments. In the meantime, lyrics for a new song were born:

Roses With No Color

You told me that you loved me
I believed every single word
You held my hand and kissed my lips
And asked me to be your girl

But now I'm blinded by a darkened cloud
The rain came streaking my face like a clown
And now I'm left with memories
Most faded in the dark
I should have seen it coming
When your roses had no color
All those useless words with no meaning
All the signs of broken dreams

You told me that you loved me
I believed every single word
You held my hand and kissed my lips
I felt like a lucky girl

With time that passed so slowly
My pride erased the pain
The rain that streaked my face that day
No longer makes me blue
But I still remember what you said
Those tender days were true

You told me that you loved me.

Dina suggested I see a therapist. Perhaps talking to someone about my grief could help. I made an appointment with her psychiatrist. I'd never had counseling before, so I wasn't familiar with the different types of mental health professionals.

My appointment was in an office on the Upper West Side. The space was an apartment/office. There was a sign on the door that said, "Enter, the door is open." I entered a semi-dark room with old Asian carpets on the floor. There were big, bell-shaped shades with small green crystals hanging from the lower rim of the table lamps that dimly lit the large room. Wooden beams anchored the high ceiling, and darker wood lined the frame of the hallway that led to a private area. The walls were lined with paintings of big red and yellow peonies, their colors dull, as if they'd been hanging there for fifty years. It made me think of my white roses, the ones with no color.

A tall woman with long, grayish hair tied into a side ponytail, wearing a brown ribbon and a multicolored knitted shawl, walked into the room holding a teacup. She introduced herself and asked me to take a seat. There were a couple of upholstered easy chairs and a navy velvet sofa with worn-out spots on the seat and arms. I chose an easy chair angled toward her with a very large wooden coffee table between us. As she put her teacup on the saucer, she asked what brought me in. I shared what I was going through, and after a few minutes, the tears started rolling down my cheeks. She passed me a box of tissues as I continued to talk, beginning to feel some relief as the minutes rolled into almost an hour.

She finally suggested that she could prescribe some medication, but that it was difficult because people react differently to the side effects. She offered some samples to start with and said that, in time, we could settle on a prescription. I accepted her pills but already felt a sense of relief as I left her office.

That afternoon, I took one of the pills. It helped me relax while I was reading a magazine, and I fell asleep while reading an article about Barbra Streisand and a tough business decision she was contending with.

When I woke up sixteen hours later, it was late afternoon. I felt groggy, and my eyes took a while to adjust to the bright daylight. I had this sense of urgency to shake off the sluggishness. Engaging in some self-talk, I said, "You can't be taking any pills that will interfere with your ability to keep up with the focus needed to succeed. You can't let yourself get depressed. You've got to stand tall."

Then I remembered the article and Ms. Streisand's words: "No matter what, the show must go on!"

I grabbed the pill pack and opened the window to my eighth-floor apartment, sending it flying out, landing on the roof of the townhouse below, as I shouted, "I don't need any pills! I can do this! My show *will* go on!"

> *There are moments when all you can do*
> *is tie the laces of your boots, lift your head,*
> *and walk forward—because the show must go on.*

CHAPTER 10

Dad and My College Education

The show did go on. My passion for performing was more potent than the love I had for someone who had other plans that didn't include me. With no pills and carrying my guardian angel on my left shoulder, I managed to have everything in place for a fantastic show, and my red dress with a train looked fabulous on me. Though some people didn't believe I could pull it off, I did. For that, I thank the conductor Francisco Zumaque, who rehearsed the band to perfection, and the cellist, Akua Dixon, and her sister, Gale, who helped put together an orchestra of forty musicians. It had been two years since the idea had begun, and now it was over.

I could return to focusing on the Mujeres Latinas® project and healing a broken heart by keeping busy. While searching for opportunities to promote the website, which now featured profiles of Latinas to serve as a tool for those women seeking mentors and role models, I visited a friend who was an administrator at Hostos Community College in the Bronx. I introduced her to the website and the concept. She liked it.

I was fortunate to have approached her at that time because she had a grant to create a program through the No Child Left Behind initiative. She offered me a twelve-week workshop and asked me to choose a book to use as the curriculum. I was so thrilled to have the opportunity. It was something new for me. I had been teaching private voice lessons, but never a group of young girls about how to develop a productive lifestyle. It would be a challenge, and it would be exciting. I always enjoyed teaching, even if it was informally.

I looked at the available books, but instead, I asked her for the opportunity to create my own workbook for the class. I wanted to include conversations that I would have with my own daughters, if I had them. I thought, *This is great.* Now I had the opportunity to fill a missing link—guiding young girls as a mentor or role model, drawing on my experiences as a mother in my forties who had many of my own experiences to share in planning a successful lifestyle.

I had three months before the workshop would begin, and I assured the director that I would have the book ready in time.

I had already planned to visit my parents in Texas, so I stayed a little longer to prepare and begin writing the workbook. I had never written a book before, but once I finished, my friends Michelle and Vincent helped me edit and design it. They are experts, and the result was a beautiful workbook titled *The Young Woman's Empowerment Journal.* I was so proud to have accomplished it, but I couldn't have done it without my team of experts.

Once it was completed, I quickly had it printed and brought the workbook to the college. Everyone involved was happily surprised that it was ready in time to start the classes. I worked through the twelve weeks of the workshop and had a wonderful time with the students. They seemed pleased running through the exercises, beginning by creating a family tree and identifying behavioral, educational, and communicational habits within their family members to understand better their family dynamics and how to manage them.

We discussed educational and career choices by first exploring each participant's family and then examining individuals who had made a positive impression on them, whom they sought out as role models. We took turns reading out loud to encourage and empower them as speakers. The students came from five high schools in the Bronx, who signed up for the credited class, coming together in the college classroom environment, creating a bridge as a natural decision for continuing their education into higher education.

To complete my students' experience with my program, I took them on an outing to the design offices of the Dominican fashion designer Oscar de La Renta. I had been in touch with his office to see if I could borrow a dress for the strings concert. Unfortunately, I couldn't use it because the way it was cut—I couldn't extend my ribcage to breathe properly while singing. However, I took the opportunity to ask if I could bring my class to his atelier, and the girls were very excited when I shared the news.

A week later, we were on the subway heading to the garment district on 7th Avenue, where his atelier was located. As we walked into the building, I immediately began pointing out the various types of personnel who make a clothing design shop operate. I pointed out the receptionist, then into the showroom, where well-dressed sales ladies were showing dresses off the rack to customers, mostly buyers for the large, high-end department stores. We then took the stairs to the second floor, where we walked past a model wearing a half-sewn, soft blue silk gown created by assistant designers working for Mr. de la Renta. In the next room, several seamstresses sewed crystals onto the train of a cranberry red mini dress. They were all smiling and seemed excited by our visit as they said hello.

As we continued around the hallway, we passed two rooms filled with colorful rolls of beautiful fabrics of various textures. We passed a tiny kitchen, where the rich aroma of freshly brewed coffee filled the air, stimulating my taste buds. I walked behind the group, along with the shyest student from the class. Just the day before, when it was her turn to talk about a job she could see herself working at, she shrugged her shoulders and shook her head when I asked, "Don't you have anything in mind—a dream, a thought, an idea?"

All the girls in class were surprised she didn't have anything in mind.

But now, as she and I poked our heads into a dark room filled with designers working at their computers, we saw a screen displaying the most beautiful emerald-green, silky high heels, decorated with an emerald stone surrounded by small crystals to complete the design. Our eyes opened wide in surprise as we both turned to each other and burst out, "Wow."

Her eyes lit up as she stood taller, and a big smile spread across her face as she said, "My father works with computers."

I hugged her. I was thrilled that this opportunity opened her mind to a world of possibilities. All the girls were so excited to meet Oscar de la Renta, who stepped out of his conference room to greet us. He autographed each picture while answering some questions from the students. We said our goodbyes and thanked everyone as Mr. de la Renta had to take a call from another important designer. Even he seemed excited by our visit. It was a memorable outing to end the twelve weeks.

Now I had to find more opportunities to run the workshop and expand the minds of young people who wouldn't otherwise have a chance to explore what could be in their future. I listed the book in the Department of Education of NYC resources and began to reach out to a couple of educators who might be interested in running the workshop. I would get excited after a meeting, but when I returned for a second one, I was turned down.

After three rejections, I shared my experience with a social worker, and she said, "You're practicing counseling without a degree."

I realized then that perhaps I wasn't being offered the opportunity because I didn't have a college degree.

That's when I decided it was time to register for college. A friend mentioned a program for adults where I could earn credits for my experiences. By this time, I was in my late forties and had enough experience that could equate to a college education. All my knowledge of musical theory, vocal training, music performances in various ensembles, including the business of music, my three languages, the history of Mexico and Brazil, and even credits for my empowerment journal—these would all count.

By identifying all the classes from a college catalog and matching them with my experiences, writing a paper for each class credit explaining my knowledge and experience, and then completing face-to-face interviews with professors for each class, I was able to rack up ninety-six credits. Now, all I had to do was complete the final thirty-six academic credits. In a year and a half, I earned my bachelor's degree. I hadn't been in school since graduating from high school in 1971, and now, in 2006, I was fifty-three years old.

I had to slow down my musical career to focus on completing the remaining classes and graduating. I even had to work with a tutor to learn algebra which I never used. I truly enjoyed gaining the knowledge, and I passed all of my classes. I got back to working on the website, focusing on securing gigs with the girl band, and working part-time at Credit Suisse to start paying off my school loans. "Oh brother!" as an elder lady friend from The South would say.

Even with state aid, I still had a substantial amount of money to pay off those student loans. Things got more complicated when I received a call from my sister, informing me that my father wasn't well.

After working as a singer, performing with the Mujeres Latinas band, teaching the workshop with my workbook in hand, managing the website, and planning to use my bachelor's degree to launch new workshops, I had to stop everything to go home to Texas and help my dad. He had been battling prostate cancer for many years, but now it was a tumor on his kidney. It was decided that instead of undergoing dialysis, the doctors would remove the kidney. I felt I was the right person to be there for him. Every one of my siblings had a full-time job, and I was the only one who was a freelancer and could leave my son in NYC to take care of the rent of my apartment. My son had now graduated and was back home, producing music for commercials.

When I arrived in Texas, I had no savings, as I had been focused on school and had just started working. I didn't even have enough money to pay for my phone bill, which was crucial since I might get a call for a singing gig that could set me up for a few months. I couldn't sing while in Texas because the only musicians in town were already part of a band, and they weren't about to cancel one of their own gigs to come work with me. I couldn't get a full-time job because I was there to take care of my dad and my mother, who had dementia. She no longer cooked and had to be taken care of, as well.

I tried cleaning apartments a couple of times until someone recognized me as the singer who performed in the Texas Jazz Festival the year before. I figured that wasn't the best publicity. The only option left was to go back to school. I had to be home anyway, and I could get a higher education loan for a master's degree student to stay afloat.

That's how I survived for about a year, accumulating a lot of school debt, until I had to drop out of school for a term because I couldn't focus or find the motivation to study. The cancer had spread, and my dad needed my attention full-time. I called the school to ask for a deferment and explained what I was going through. Mid-sentence, the tears started to roll down my face. The young man on the other end said, "I understand what you're going through. It must be very difficult for you. Do you mind if we take a moment so I may pray for you?"

The tears didn't stop as I said, "Please do."

As he prayed, I reflected on my own life—on putting my career on hold along with all my projects. I was studying when I should have been singing and working. I worried about my apartment in New York City. I worried about the rent and other small bills I had, but I was glad I was there for my family. His prayer, with each word, helped to slow each tear down until I could finally take a deep breath. I felt so relieved and so loved in that moment by my peer. I had been feeling very lonely in those final weeks of my father's life, but as I heard him pray for me, I felt loved. The prayer and the love gave me the strength to carry on. He assured me that my education would be there waiting for me whenever I was ready. I felt a huge weight lifted from my chest.

The next few months were challenging as I watched my dad, whom I loved dearly, slowly lose his appetite. I tried to find foods I could cook that would be appetizing. I thought about our Sunday calls, which had become a habit because I lived so far away. I reflected on the time when he and my mom came to NYC to visit me, and how I had him taking taxis to meet me so I could take them sightseeing—the Statue of Liberty, dinner at the Rainbow Room where I had worked, the South Street Seaport to see the ships, and a jazz club to see me sing.

I also recalled that when I had first arrived from New York, he was still strong. I caught him dancing in the living room by himself as he listened to his favorite bolero from a Toña La Negra album. My mother would be watching him as she sat on her swing on the back porch. After dinner, he would call my mother to come join him and watch the soccer games. I even caught them smooching on the sofa, something that was very unusual, as my parents were reserved about showing affection in public. My mother would call him a sourpuss because she didn't mind the affection, but I think it had to do with their native culture. Another time, as I was preparing lunch and looking out the kitchen window, I spied on him swinging his golf club in the backyard, just entertaining himself since he could no longer drive himself anywhere.

It was heartbreaking. Nothing I prepared seemed appetizing. I tried making foods he could eat—dishes with minimal seasoning such as pureed greens, scrambled eggs, a boiled potato, yogurt, and milkshakes—but nothing worked. It was his body giving up.

I remember my father's last days clearly. He never wanted the morphine. Instead, he asked me for a little shot of red wine he kept in a cabinet. Only a day later in the evening, before my sister left for work, she leaned over to kiss him, saying, "I'm going off to work. I'll see you in the morning."

I walked out with her to lock the front door, then joined my mother on the sofa in the living room. She was watching television. I don't believe she understood that my dad was in his final days. She was in a dementia fog and seemed disconnected during those last days. After a few minutes, I went back into the bedroom to check on him. He was lying there quietly, tapping his chest. I bent over to kiss him on the forehead as he took his last breath and closed his eyes.

Life passes too quickly. Don't wait for tomorrow to give a hug or make a call to someone you love.

CHAPTER 11

A New Love, A New Life

After my dad passed away, I returned to NYC and made an agreement with my sister: she would stop working to care for our mother, while I would take on the responsibility of paying the bills. I completed my master's degree in 2011 and began working as a mental health counselor in Upper Manhattan at a local clinic. I needed to fulfill 3,500 hours of work—about three years of clinical experience—before I could sit for the licensing test.

I wasn't singing much anymore, mainly because I didn't want the hassle of organizing a band, especially since my job prevented me from leaving town, and I had a new weekend relationship. I had worked so many weekends singing that now I was enjoying other activities. As a friend said, "She's encantada de la vida."

So yes, I was enchanted with a new romance and delighted to be free to enjoy it.

At the clinic, I was still working toward completing my license, but I was already earning a steady income and truly enjoying my work—and my weekends. In addition to seeing clients individually, I also ran group sessions. One of my youngest clients, a five-year-old boy, was brought in by his mother, who said she couldn't get him or his seven-year-old sister to sit still. She suspected they had attention deficit disorder (ADD). When I asked the boy what was going on at home, he told me that his mother owned a small dog that was constantly barking, making him feel "crazy." Despite his frustration, his mother refused to get rid of the dog.

On the opposite end of the spectrum, my oldest client was a ninety-four-year-old woman in my seniors' women's group. She suffered from depression and was forced to sleep in a recliner in the living room while her granddaughter had the extra bedroom. The stress from this situation affected her health—she wasn't getting enough rest. She told me she couldn't fall asleep before 2:00 a.m. because her grandson in the other bedroom played loud music, and she had to wake up at 6:00 a.m. She lived in constant fear because her daughter threatened to throw her out if she didn't wake up on time, make her bed, and help with the morning routine. She would often end up at the local senior center to get some rest in a recliner there.

Cases like these taught me the importance of family social skills. Helping family members respect each other's need for space, privacy, and quiet moments can make a big difference in overall well-being. While it's true that poverty often leads to shared living spaces, I was able to help my elderly client find an apartment in a senior living facility, which brought her the peace she desperately needed. She was also working on improving her mental health by continuing to attend my group sessions, where she received support from the other women, which played a significant role in her positive changes.

Improving communication within families is key. Encouraging activities like cooking together, playing card or board games, and setting clear boundaries can help reduce conflict. Active listening, empathy, and being observant of each other's needs can prevent combative behavior and create a healthier environment for everyone. Family therapy can also help open lines of communication and address underlying issues.

In my work as a mental health therapist, I've seen that many people living with conditions like schizophrenia, ADHD, OCD, and other mental health challenges often rely on medication to manage their symptoms and live productive lives. But I've also learned that medication alone isn't enough. For example, poor parenting or a lack of support can complicate matters, social skills and helping families recognize mental health struggles early on can help them navigate difficult situations. This applies not only to family dynamics but also to romantic relationships.

What may start as a strong connection with someone who seems like a 'soul mate' can sometimes shift dramatically if mental health challenges arise. That's when things can get sticky, making it difficult to break free from a troubled relationship. If you or someone you know is facing mental health struggles, being proactive about seeking help is essential. A diagnosis can provide clarity and be the first step toward healing.

At the clinic, I made steady progress toward completing my required hours, taking on as many cases as I could manage. On weekends, I would take a break from counseling to listen to live music performances. In the past, I had been a performer myself, but now I could sit in the audience and simply enjoy the show.

After a concert, I would usually go backstage to say hello to musicians I knew. It was at a Latin jazz concert that I was introduced to a very tall, handsome gentleman backstage by Xiomara, a family friend whose father was performing that evening. As it was time to leave, a group of us walked out toward our cars. I felt as if the stars had aligned that night, as I was in the right place at the right time. Xiomara had dashed off to meet some friends, so I was able to walk and talk with Bob. Not only was he very tall and handsome, but he was a casually respectful gentleman—the kind of guy a woman dreams of.

As we got to know each other over the next few years, we discovered many things we had in common. We knew many of the same people who were part of the groups of musicians and friends we both connected with. We also shared a love for good food with family and friends. We were both raised with American culture, but also loved Latin music, and he lived in Pennsylvania, where my mother was born. I did introduce him to more Latin food besides his favorite *chile relleno* (a green poblano chile stuffed with cheese) and pork carnitas in a light tomato salsa. I still kid him, saying it was my mother who brought the stars into alignment for us.

After seeing each other for a couple of years, one day, Bob came to see me in New York and simply said, "Hey, let's get married. I can get you a car so you can finish your second year at the clinic and come home on the weekends."

It sounded like a good arrangement, but at sixty years old, I didn't think much about getting married again. I just thought about the stars aligning the night we met. I would work four days a week and then come home to my husband on Thursday evenings. On Mondays, I would return to NYC to work by early afternoon. Somehow, I forgot about singing on the weekends, which had been my original plan had I not met this wonderful man.

In May 2014, we walked into the local magisterial district court in New Hope and got married by the district judge. You could say we eloped, as my son Billy said when we shared the news with him, and only with him. My son, who lived on the West Coast, had already met Bob during a vacation we took to introduce him to the family. During that first trip in April, Bob told my son he would marry me, but never said when, so it was a bit of a surprise when we shared that we got married. I should have written a poem titled *"We Married in May."* It's never too late to start. And it's never too late to get married—as I said, I was sixty.

We had our wedding celebration in August, with our family and friends, and had my young granddaughters as the flower girls. It was a beautiful ceremony under a delicate lace umbrella that Xiomara held over me while we exchanged our vows, all beneath a light sprinkle of rain. The Latin music started, the dancers took the floor, and the feast began under a big white tent at a family estate in Bucks County, surrounded by stone farmhouses, beautiful gardens with colorful dahlias and wildflowers, and cornfields beyond the flowers. You could see horses grazing on rolling green knolls in the distance. I recall being incredibly happy that day.

By the time I completed all my clinic hours, we had already been married for a year. My husband was running his business, so the busy schedule worked fine for us. Coming home on the weekends was enough without having to go out. I was already living in a pleasant town. We enjoyed our time taking vacations, dining at restaurants in search of good food, and occasionally visiting a jazz club to catch up with friends who were performing. With my hours completed, I gave up my apartment in NYC to live full-time in Bucks County.

I must admit, it took some time to adjust to being surrounded by tall evergreens, mountains, and winding roads. Our neighbors live an acre away, and most homes are hidden from view by long driveways that wind deep into the woods. I often see deer crossing the roads as I drive, or bucks hiding from hunters in my backyard during the fall. In the spring and summer, there are rabbits, raccoons walking through the yard looking for food, a groundhog, snakes, and a giant hawk hunting for a rabbit. Just the other day, I saw a beautiful red fox walk along the fence with its full, fluffy tail pointing straight out as if it owned the yard. I'm surprised it didn't have a few chicken feathers stuck around its nose, since I know that's what it was coming to search for at the property behind us. I used to hear their rooster, but not lately.

Yes, there are plenty of bright red cardinals, squawking blue jays, red-winged blackbirds, red-headed woodpeckers, hummingbirds, and doves. Occasionally, a whole murder of black crows (as a group of those birds is called) lands in the backyard, enjoying our wide-open space. I've seen wild turkeys along back roads. I've also seen big black vultures eating roadkill, but not in our backyard. On a couple of occasions, I have stopped on a back road to help a turtle cross the road to avoid being hit by a passing car.

I only see people when I go into town to shop or just drive around, because I need to see others. Even if it's just talking to a saleslady or a shopper in the parking lot, I'll comment on the weather or the idiot who didn't push their shopping cart back where it belongs. I know we have neighbors because I occasionally hear gunshots—likely practice for deer hunting season. We even enjoy our own Fourth of July fireworks from two of our neighbors. I try to have parties and invite friends from NYC, but no one has a car, and it's just no fun to drive back and forth in one day. When I visit friends in New York City, I usually stay overnight and catch up on the city's nightlife. I used to miss it a lot, but not as much now, especially since the pandemic.

And besides, NYC just doesn't feel the same. Not like when I arrived in '74 and sang and hung out at jazz clubs that were open till 3:00 or 4:00 in the morning through the '70s, '80s. By the late '90s, the city was quiet by 2:00 a.m. After the tragedy of 9/11, the scene started to change even more, with some clubs even closing at 1:00 a.m. and with a stricter noise curfew. So, staying closer to home was fine because I now had new interests, such as writing and maintaining my website. Additionally, we found that after trying out numerous restaurants in the area, we enjoy home cooking the best.

There are plenty of good ingredients to shop for at the local farm stands—fresh garden produce, meats, and I love the local turkey dogs. Where I once purchased flowers, I now head to my backyard and pick the bright, fiery burnt-orange Mexican sunflowers and the delicate pastel colors of the cosmos—both my favorites—among the Shasta daisies, and not to leave out the white, purple, and yellow callas that performed so well last summer.

My life still involves a fair amount of traveling—usually vacations to destinations around the world—since I haven't been singing much, due to the long distances required to reach a venue. My husband hasn't traveled as much as I have, so he's thoroughly enjoying our vacations together, with our next one planned to Panama City and Cartagena, Colombia. That will get me to over forty countries I have visited.

He's also a very good fisherman, so I get to eat fresh fish several times a year. I've even learned to identify the fish by name when I go to the fish market to restock our supply, which we freeze. When he fishes, I write, read, or wander along the shore, singing and looking for small, colorful shells. I run back when he calmly shouts out, "I got another one!" to see if it's a flounder, a grouper, a striped bass, or my favorite to make ceviche—fresh mangrove snapper that I marinate in lime with red onion rings and chopped cilantro.

It's a fun and exciting time when we have the summer vacation all together. Bob especially loves it when he has all the grandkids fishing. We still must get Miles Jr. into the fishing group. But they all have a blast with him, and they call him "Grandpa."

Bob and I love cooking together for a large crowd, and we laugh a lot because he's great at quick one-liner jokes. We also quiz each other on lyrics from pop songs we grew up with. To avoid criticizing one another, we say, "You're funny."

It really works well; it stops any argument that might be brewing—you

should try it. All in all, we make a pretty good couple, even though he's 6'5"
and I'm 5'3".

You're never too old to remarry
when you've found real love.

CHAPTER 12

Grandma to the Rescue

After working as a therapist in my new home state of Pennsylvania, I decided to put that job on hold due to the amount of driving required along the back roads of Bucks and Montgomery Counties to reach my clients. Besides, my husband said a couple of times, "You don't have to work, you know."

I thought about it. I'm someone who enjoys staying active and having my own money to spend, so I decided to start collecting my Social Security. I finally made it.

I was never much of a homemaker. I'm not big on decorating the house for the holidays or baking pies, but I try to keep things in order, so I don't have to spend a lot of time putting things back in their place. Yes, occasionally I'll pull out my sewing machine to mend some items. I do the laundry every day, so it doesn't pile up. I enjoy looking out the picture window to see what's visiting our lawn while I fold a load.

I collect a lot of notes, music sheets, lyrics, magazines, and books, so we definitely have a lived-in space. I also help cook the meals and clean up after dinner, but my mind is often on my projects or a lyric. I take breaks from my computer to sit with my husband to watch a movie or start a new series. Series are trouble for me because once I start one, I don't want to stop until I get to the end. But once it's over, I'm back at my computer working on my projects.

I work on keeping up my mujereslatinas.com website, writing new profiles, adding fresh pictures, upgrading the site, and seeking help from my two assistants, Sandra and Brianna. We all work from our home office due to the distance between us, since they live in New Jersey.

Now that I have more time, I find it exciting again to discover women who are being brought out of the archives. Their books and articles have been hiding somewhere on the back shelves of government or university libraries. Now, their stories were coming to light as curious minds research old collections of books. These books told the stories of heroines, feminists, educators, and artists with political slants—some who had to leave their countries in fear of prosecution, while others returned when it was safe again. These women had limited print runs, little distribution, and minimal promotion, with most books staying local, not crossing borders. The few early books on feminism were shelved. These Latinas could have been introduced to, broader audiences, serving as role models and mentors, other than Hollywood actresses and popular music artists who have been fed to us, limiting our intellectual development and starving inquisitive minds from discovering the world beyond.

When I found the story of the Afro-Argentine soldier and heroine Manuela Remedios del Valle, I added her profile to the website. I was so surprised to learn that she had been called the "mother of Argentina" by her comrades in the war due to her dedication to fighting for Argentina's independence from Spain. And yet, her story only became publicized as women today seek out their heroines—role models who inspire motivation and challenge the possibilities for curious women.

Today, more stories are emerging from the hidden, dusty corners of bookcases. In these times, women are making their mark in public service, business, science, sports, entertainment, journalism, on television, and even producing their own podcasts. They are out there, we just need to highlight them more to encourage young women to seek role models and mentors, further empowering them to pursue higher education and explore varied career paths they may not have been exposed to. Finally, I can focus on the website project I started in 1997. In the past, I had to divide my time between earning money to pay rent, being lured to travel and sing, and taking care of my family when needed. But there's no giving up—we continue to help spread the profiles to reach curious minds.

I was working on a profile when I was told we were going on vacation. *I thought, no problem—I can get back to the website when we return. I could use the vacation to catch up on reading more about heroic women in the world.*

We landed at the airport located on top of a mountain near the capital city of San José, Costa Rica. In a rented car, we took Highway 34, which brought us down along the beach towns until we reached our destination near the Manuel Antonio State Park. It's on the western shoreline of a beautiful white sand beach. Our small boutique hotel was fifty yards from Coco Beach, which forms a semicircle that hugs the shore. The soft, warm waves invite you into the crystal-clear water to swim as long as you like. Or you could lie on a lounger reading while the aroma of freshly caught and grilled snapper drifts over from the nearby bar, luring you to sit up and eat.

It's a place where you just want to keep swimming, eating, and reading for days. I'd like to go back, but I wish they had an airport closer to the beach without the three-hour travel time.

When we returned home, it was the end of February, and within a day, Bob said he wasn't feeling well and stayed in bed for a week. That's when the news broke about the virus. I only had mild cold symptoms that lasted two or three days, but it took Bob two weeks to recover. We hadn't heard much about COVID-19, but after Bob got better, we thought we might have been exposed to it at the airport on our return. As weeks went by and cases began to be reported, we had no doubt it was COVID-19, because Bob hadn't experienced anything like those symptoms or the extreme fatigue. Being seniors, we were fortunate it wasn't tragic. Still, we started watching the news about the large numbers of people getting sick, having breathing problems, and how the hospitals were becoming overwhelmed.

The lockdown began by mid-March, and people started wearing masks and gloves, with some even covering their shoes when they went outside. Each week, more people stayed home, only going out for groceries and washing everything down once they returned. It was a terrifying time and devastating to lose family members and friends who did not survive COVID-19, which is believed to have started in 2019.

By May 2020, some states began to ease restrictions, but a resurgence occurred in the South and West, which was believed to have contributed to the continued spread of the SARS-CoV-2 virus (Severe Acute Respiratory Syndrome Coronavirus 2). People began stepping out of their homes, trying to continue their lives as work was interrupted, schools were closed, and people were tired of staying indoors, especially in big cities where apartments can be small.

Over the next few months, the virus continued to take its toll, primarily on people with preexisting health conditions. By mid-August, my daughter-in-law was planning to give birth in September. She was expecting her second child, a boy, and was scheduled to give birth on September 4.

A few weeks before her due date, my son called and asked if I could come to help, since he was extremely busy with work and, with the schools closed, they needed help taking care of their firstborn, who was about three years old at the time. When I asked my husband, he said, "No way, you're not getting on a plane."

So, I didn't push the issue until September 4 arrived and the baby was born. On the third day, my son called, demanding I get on a plane immediately to help, because there was no one he could hire due to the virus still resurging in various cities. He couldn't keep up with his work and running his business, and he couldn't find anyone to hire because of the order to stay indoors.

When I told my husband I had to go and help my son, again he said, "Oh, no! You're not going anywhere!"

I tried to explain that this was family, and they needed me because my daughter-in-law had had a cesarean, and it would take six to eight weeks for her recovery. He said it again, "No!"

I stood my ground and explained that it was a cultural thing. "In my culture, grandmothers always come to the rescue," I said, looking him in the eye, "and you're funny!"

He looked at me, then said, "Okay, but you need to get a hazmat suit."

I said, "Don't worry, I don't want to get anyone sick, especially a baby. And there's no time to get a suit. I'll wrap myself up."

I booked the flight for the next day and immediately searched for something to wear as a safety suit. We had some plastic drop cloths used for protecting floors and furniture, so I used scissors to cut out the shape of pants, then taped up and sealed the inside and outside of the legs. I wrapped a belt around my waist to hold up the plastic pants, which I wore over my sweatpants. For the top, I had a plastic hooded rain poncho that I travel with in case it rains when I'm on a small boat during fishing trips. I wore it over a hoodie and taped all sides of the plastic poncho to ensure I was sealed in, with a second belt tied around the waist so I could use the bathroom, because when you have to go, no matter what, you have to go.

When I walked through the airport, I had to pass security. I was surprised they let me through without removing my plastic suit, but a security dog had already sniffed me when I first stepped into the airport. People looked at me, but I never heard a laugh or saw any reaction. I didn't see anyone, but I had heard that a famous model had been spotted wearing a hazmat suit a few days before.

I was finally seated in my first-class seat, which my husband had purchased so I could disembark from the plane quickly. Additionally, they were offering discounts due to the decline in travel resulting from the virus. When we arrived and stood in the aisle, some folks looked at me, and I said, "I'm going to care for my newborn grandson, so I'm trying my best to protect myself and my family."

No one said anything, except for the couple seated behind me, who whispered to each other, "Perhaps we should have worn a mask at least."

As we disembarked the plane, I went down to the main floor to recover my plastic-wrapped luggage, then stepped outside where my son was waiting. I quickly stripped myself of all the plastic suit and the luggage as well, rolled it up, and placed it in the trash can. Minutes later, I was safely in the car as my son hugged me and said, "Thanks, Mom, we really need you."

When family calls—and you have the will—
you'll always find the way.

CHAPTER 13

National School of the Arts of Cuba

We managed to survive COVID-19, and the world began to return to its routines, though with some caution. Most people received several doses of the vaccine against the SARS virus, while seniors continued to wear their masks. Many people never left home without a hand sanitizer in their pocket, and they maintained a safe distance during conversations. There were no hugs or kisses during greetings; instead, people would lean in for an elbow tap, which became the new standard for the moment.

As soon as I heard anyone coughing around me, I would pull my mask up over my nose and mouth, and I didn't back off until the COVID casualties slowed down. I'd use my sleeve or carry a scarf to use when I had to open a door. I kept gloves in my car to pump gas. With the virus and others predicted for the near future, I thought I wouldn't be singing anymore. It had been almost a decade since my last gig, and the distance to New York City was still an issue, especially if there wasn't a budget to put me up in a hotel. And besides, I hadn't vocalized in many years. There were new warnings that another virus might be on the way soon. I had already caught COVID toward the end of the run, and it had taken me several weeks to feel fully recovered. The lingering symptoms—especially the horrible phlegm—made it impossible to sing a high note with a clear, steady sound. So yes, you think twice before setting yourself up for that kind of disaster.

But life moved on. Students returned to school, which made it official. Everything started to feel more normal, and life resumed its normal course.

COVID made it comfortable to stay close to home and stay busy with gardening, or writing, my new interest. I had a website, still a work in progress, and had started taking writing classes to learn how to build a better story. I had five expired passports filled with stamps of places I had visited, each one attached to a memory. I was enjoying the classes and the writers, whose tales were so varied. Some were rich in expression, seeking an audience as they read from their pages. Other writers' stories were so dry that not only were they learning to bring their words to life, but they were also learning to express those words when reading aloud. At times, it felt like not just a writing class, but an acting class for expression and delivery.

I was enjoying writing my stories and reviewing poetry I had written over the years. I thought, *Okay, writing has become a part of who I am.* Just when I thought I wouldn't be singing again, I received a call from a professor at the National School of the Arts in Cuba. He asked to interview me about one of my early music teachers from 1977. He was preparing his thesis and needed all the information he could find. I shared with Professor Janio Abreu Morcate that Maestro Alberto Socarrás had arrived from Cuba around 1925 and was possibly the first Cuban flautist in the world to record a solo.

Maestro Socarrás was also the first Cuban to perform at the Apollo Theater, billed as "Alberto Socarrás and his Magic Flute." As a master of wind instruments, he performed at New York City local clubs like the Cotton Club and the Savoy, and he very likely performed his solo from Clarence

Williams's recording of "Shooting the Pistol." He was also known as the bandleader who rehearsed members of Anacaona, an all-female orchestra, in which my mentor Graciela Grillo played bass and sang. Graciela helped complete the band's contract to perform in Europe, which also had its own stories.

During my music lessons, which usually lasted about fifteen minutes—just enough time to recite my homework—Maestro Socarrás would begin to recollect stories of his performances, the nightclubs of his day, and how poorly music was taught in the US. I'm not sure I agree with that. Still, I do remember hearing from my old boss Mario Bauzá. Maestro Socarrás and Bebo Valdés said that to be a true Master of Music, one had to pass through the symphony orchestra to complete their musical education. What is known about Cuban education is that studies of any kind are taught with greater intensity, involving many more hours of practice focused on the instrument, without the need to work to pay for your education, right up to the doctoral level.

The Maestro shared with me that he had stopped performing and dedicated himself to writing musical arrangements for the acts of his day, including Cab Calloway and Benny Carter, and also served as an arranger for the Latin music department at Columbia Records. Later, he taught music lessons using the *Solfeo* technique to students like me.

He lived in a brownstone building, up one flight of stairs, where I would occasionally cross paths with another student leaving his studio on West 54th Street. He lived in the past with a quiet pride surrounded by his awards, pictures, music books, stacks of musical arrangements, and instrument cases. I'm sure one of them contained his magic flute.

After my phone interview with Professor Morcate, I offered to send him my musical arrangements of some Cuban masters, which had been collecting dust in my closet from my time performing with Mario Bauzá and the Afro-Cuban Jazz Orchestra. He said he would love to have copies and that he would rehearse his school orchestra so I could come to Cuba to perform with his students. Not having sung in over ten years, I couldn't believe I would be offered such a great opportunity, and at just months away from turning seventy.

It's well-known that students at the National School of the Arts of Cuba are incredibly well-trained and excellent musicians. While in high school, they study their art five days a week, for the entire day. That surprise phone call became the fork in the road that created another adventure in my life. Of course, I accepted. It would be an honor to perform with the members of his high school orchestra.

It was 2023 when I traveled to Cuba with my husband to give three concerts—two at the Martí Theater, a historic venue that has undergone a couple of renovations since its construction in the late 1800s. Despite the changes, it still retains the beauty and fine finesse of its colonial period, which ended in 1898. The other concert was at the Art Factory of Cuba (FAC), an old factory converted into a large art and music space. It features rooms of various sizes where performances take place simultaneously, and it fills up with people of all ages.

Cuba is restoring many of their old colonial façades, integrating new construction to create hotels. There was a lot of construction happening during this stay—old mansions being restored and transformed into beautiful restaurants, decorated with artifacts that have either survived over the years or been restored in creative ways. Some items were repurposed simply by flipping a cracked decorative pot to serve as a base for a smaller potted flower or using old wood-sculpted doors as wall decorations. The collection of fine dinner plates, glasses, and dinnerware was a mix of old and new patterns and colors, creatively combined into something artistic. In Cuba, nothing goes to waste. Everything that can be restored is, cutting away what's truly unusable, while scraps are used artistically as filler for empty spaces.

We had traveled to Cuba in 2017 for a brief trip while President Obama was still in office, and this had made it possible for us to engage in cultural exchanges. There was no construction going on then, and I didn't see any local people with cell phones on the street. There were plenty of tourists, with large crowds at the most popular tourist bars and cafés. The constant rolling of bright, colorful, old American classic cars, many convertibles driving up and down *El Malecón* or along the promenade, would park outside the hotels, waiting for their next customers. You could feel the hope among the Cuban community that perhaps there would be positive changes.

Now, in 2023, the changes were evident—new hotels, restaurants, nightlife, and plenty of talented musicians playing around every corner in Old Havana, at the main tourist spots, and in a few cities. However, due to COVID-19 still circulating, tourism was light, and once again, the community wondered what the future would bring.

Some restrictions had been lifted, allowing shops to bring in containers of goods that would quickly sell out until the next delivery arrived. Goods from Canada and Spain, including new clothing and shoes, had started to arrive, though they were still in short supply. I saw young males wearing crisp, shiny new sneakers, new jeans, and knock-off designer T-shirts. Some young people walked around, looking down at their cell phones. One shop I walked into looking for snacks was a real surprise—I found cans of Coca-Cola, crackers, and personal hygiene items like toothpaste and even soap, which hadn't been readily available in the past. We even saw a motor scooter with a six-pack of beer in its basket—something we definitely didn't see in 2017.

Still, there were many shortages, and the lack of money meant that many Cubans could not afford the goods that had arrived. The row of colorful convertibles sat idle during this trip. The atmosphere on the street felt more liberal but still contained. On this trip, I saw fewer tourists, perhaps due to the fear of contracting COVID, which they may have feared was lingering on the island. In fact, with a population of eleven million, fewer than seven thousand people had died from the virus. The Cuban government produced their own vaccines and managed to vaccinate over ninety percent of its population. Tourists sat at outdoor cafés and in restaurants that provided good food, but they were not mingling with locals. Some restaurants had a limited menu, but it was still tasty and satisfying. Cuba seemed to be preparing for new tourism, though I couldn't help but wonder how it was all unfolding.

It was a delightful moment meeting the students for the first rehearsal. They were polite, well-mannered, and oh so curious, asking a variety of questions with smiles ear to ear. I had a wonderful time singing with these good-looking, happy, dedicated students who played instruments that had been substantially repaired, with some even donated by visiting artists.

I never thought I could get ready in time, but diligent practice paid off, and my early training helped get my voice back in shape. When you're young, it's easier, but as you get older, you don't have the same energy. However, after many years of singing, before my hiatus and the extensive training I received, my vocal cords are in pretty good shape for my age. I can still belt it out when needed. Now I was so excited about this opportunity that I pushed myself to get ready, and I did. I was ready.

The students and everyone involved were delighted because, in school, their curriculum only allowed classical music. However, they had received special permission to perform the Cuban mambo and bolero in the beloved

Martí Theater and the hip FAC warehouse. The experience was invaluable for the students, who showed up dressed in black and white, but personalized their look as best they could. Some had their hair styled in braids or perfectly shaped curls, while others wore their long, thick, shiny hair with pride, carefully styled by their proud mothers. The girls wore red lipstick and simple, fashion-forward blouses—little touches that revealed their developed taste in art. The boys, along with a couple of girls, added to the 'hip' vibe at the FAC music space by pulling out their shades.

Overall, I had a wonderful time performing with the students. One of the most memorable moments came between songs at the Martí Theater, when a woman stood up from her seat in the sixth row. She spoke about how the music brought tears to her eyes and warmed her heart, reminding her of the live performances she so dearly missed, given the prevalence of contemporary music today. Every person in the audience, as well as those behind the scenes, stepped forward for a great round of applause. The students were gleeful, as was I.

The production was a success, with everyone involved feeling content with the beautiful show and the superb performance by the high school students. You can catch some of the tunes on YouTube under Adela Dalto.

After posting some videos on social media, I was lucky to receive a call from local musicians offering me some gigs. Thanks to them, I'm still performing—not often, but enough to stay in shape, because you never know when the phone will ring with a gig somewhere in the world. I've learned to keep in shape and never lose what I've earned. Life can be long, so I'm living it to the fullest.

Now, I'm busier than ever. I sing sometimes, write for my website, give talks about my adventures in music, my travels, and the profiles of Latinas as mentors and role models. I'm writing this book and ready to start another. I take vacations with my husband to exotic places or to visit the grandkids. What more could I ask for? My husband says, "How about retiring?"

I look at him like he's being funny.

Retire? For what?
Life is for living... and for the unexpected.

CHAPTER 14

Embracing the Adventure of Life

was sitting in a salon on Madison Avenue in Manhattan, getting my hair colored. While waiting for the thirty minutes it takes to set, the colorist came over to talk to me since she wasn't busy with another client. She pulled up a chair and started chatting. We talked about where I live, her children, and our husbands. She confessed that she was getting bored with her husband's attitude, and I told her that I, too, can get bored with my husband's chatter. It's normal. She's about forty-five, and I'm seventy, so there's quite a difference in our ages.

We also discussed my singing career and the places I've traveled to. I shared that I don't perform as often as I used to. She returned to the topic of her husband, telling me that she feels like leaving him. Speaking from my own experiences, I said to her that unless she ever felt unsafe or believed he was a threat to her or their children, leaving might not be the right step. I shared how my husband and I have rekindled our relationship over the years through cooking, traveling, and watching movies together.

When children leave the nest, it opens space for fresh romance, hobbies, and interests, so I encouraged her to choose her hobbies wisely—ones that can bring fulfillment and make her happy. She then surprised me by asking, "When was the happiest time in your life?"

It struck me that, despite my age, my life is far from over. I might be older, but my life is certainly not over. As a young hair colorist with many older, grey-haired women as clients, I imagine she's heard a variety of stories. Perhaps she thinks that at seventy, my life is winding down, with no more opportunities for great times ahead. She's wrong. While she's young, her perspective is naturally different. She may be focused on romance, but I know the importance of starting a cozy fire to keep life vibrant. My life could still stretch another twenty to thirty years, and I'm ready for whatever is ahead.

I don't know what tomorrow will bring. It could be a phone call offering a singing gig somewhere in the world, or it could be news of another grandchild on the way. It could even be the thought of another fragrant red rose blooming on my favorite bush. But I know that tomorrow is my favorite time because it holds endless possibilities that keep me excited and motivated.

Many lovely surprises may come the day after that. The future is what we live for, and yesterday's memories can entertain us as we wait. It's fine to reminisce, but planning ahead offers a greater opportunity for happiness. Every joyful moment eventually ends. So, I can say that my happiest time is living for tomorrow.

What keeps me motivated is the anticipation that something great could happen. For example, today I'm getting my hair colored in preparation for what tomorrow may bring. Will I be ready for an adventure? Who wouldn't want a pleasant surprise that could come soon? Yes, I say, keep dreaming, keep planning your next adventure, and stay committed to your exercise routine. Don't let anything you've learned become rusty unless, of course, you're ready to let it go.

Experiment, try new things, and keep learning, because a surprise may present itself at any moment. The question is, will you be ready mentally, emotionally, and physically? Finish your education and training to secure that job you've been planning on. It's okay to change careers—you can always go back if you miss what you had—but be careful what you change, because you may not be able to return to a relationship.

Are there ghosts in your closet? Facing them through self-reflection or sitting with a therapist to deal with unresolved issues in your life can be daunting, but brave. Solving these mysteries will create positive endorphins, helping you feel confident and happy, which will carry you through the day and into tomorrow. Maintaining a healthy lifestyle, including regular exercise and a balanced diet, is vital for living a longer life and enjoying many more exciting adventures.

As for my travels, which now tend to be for vacation unless a phone call brings a gig (one never knows), we're planning a trip to Panama and Colombia—two countries I haven't visited. We're taking a cruise and will visit cities and beaches. To prepare, I've started exercising my upper body to carry my backpack and strengthening my legs for stairs, hills, and perhaps even a mountain. We'll see.

I encourage you not to be afraid to climb life's mountain. Test your abilities. Success isn't just about earning money; it's about the confidence you build to become a stronger person. The more confident you are, the more you attract what you want in life. Even those who may be jealous of you will secretly admire your strength. Whatever you're learning, you're not learning it for others—you're learning it for yourself, to fulfill your own needs, desires, and dreams. Sometimes, it only takes those first two or three steps to know if you're going to like what you're doing. If not, you can move on and try something different.

Never give up on what you enjoy. Even if it's just small steps, those will eventually become bigger ones until they're all yours. You may think you're done with learning for now, but you want tomorrow to be a new adventure—something exciting, something different. Look over your expenses and plan your adventures. Calculate how much you need and save toward your goal. If you know how much you need to travel, saving becomes easier. If you want it badly enough, you'll find ways to save for your adventure—and it doesn't have to be an expensive one.

Adventure begins in your neighborhood or thousands of miles away. It begins with using your five senses to fully engage with the world and perceive it as it truly is. You don't have to travel far. Whether it's just sitting and looking out a window, being mindful of anything that moves—or doesn't move—it could be a person walking a dog. You could build a mental story of where they might have come from. Or perhaps a historic building invites you to imagine its history, and who might have helped to build it or who lived there.

Learn to be attentive. Smell the aroma of spices floating out of a window as you walk down the street. Think about the culture in which those spices are used. Listen to the sounds around you. Listen to the rhythm of the community. Are they foreign voices or ear-catching melodies? Living in a city offers a diverse culture from many different countries.

You can visit community centers that often hold events celebrating particular cultures. Sometimes we forget to explore free parks, free concerts, libraries, and museums, which are full of adventures through stories, music, paintings, fashion, and even jewels. Step into a place that feels interesting, fresh, and new.

Feel the earth beneath your feet. Find a field of wildflowers, breathe deeply, and enjoy the sounds of the wind blowing through forest branches, or perhaps climb a majestic mountain. Lying on the grass, looking up at the ever-changing shapes of clouds, an adventure can be a daydream you create, filled with your favorite images somewhere far from home. Just open your mind.

We will live longer, healthier, and happier if we keep moving forward, putting one foot in front of the other, and embracing life's adventures, one stage at a time.

Acknowledgments

 $\mathcal{W}$ riting a book takes a lot of time alone—time to think, recall memories, and research to confirm what I'm sharing with my audience. It means spending hours at the computer that turn into days, then weeks, and when I was months in, I started to question myself: *Am I ever going to get to the end? I have so many stories.*

Sitting at my computer with a pen and notebook at my side, a large pitcher of water with mint and lemon, and a couple of snacks to keep me going before the next interruption, I keep writing. I still have to cook to eat, tidy up in case someone drops by, and open all the mail and emails—just in case something important comes through.

Thankfully, I had help when I needed it most, and for that, I am deeply grateful.

Thank you to my husband, Robert Moraux, who has supported me through my writing by cooking excellent meals, allowing me to stay focused and complete my manuscript. Thank you also for being a beta reader and allowing me the undisturbed time I needed to stop at just the right place, from which I could pick up again the next day, or sometimes many days later.

To Dina D'Oyen, my comadre, who always supported me in whatever projects I shared with her, and who encouraged me to keep a journal, telling me I'd have a lot to write about later. I thank you, Dina, for your sisterhood and over fifty years of friendship. And thank you for teaching me how to make the *arroz con gandules*. I'll never forget your words: "Always taste the water after the spices, before you cook it down—make sure it has a good balance of flavors." Dina, you can say that's how we lived our lives: if the flavor was there, it was meant for us.

Thank you to Darity Wesley for coaching me along the way and encouraging me to keep writing. To my editor, Valerie Costa, and her team, thank you for turning my manuscript into a printable and shareable book.

To Steve Bryant, my beta reader and first editor, and to Sofia Vento, who, after reading the first chapter, enthusiastically said, "I want to read more!"—thank you. To cousins Ruben Rocha as a beta reader and Olga Jimenez who have given me much laughter and joy just talking between chapters, thank you.

Thank you to Sandra I. Gonzalez and Brianna N. Rodriguez, my assistants in marketing and in editing my website and newsletter. You've kept the social media flowing and have supported me in more ways than one. Thank you also to Nicolasa I. Gonzalez for being a guiding light and constant source of encouragement who keeps us all moving forward. Eric Rodrigues, thank you kindly for your beautiful graphics, arriving just in time.

To my friends from Bear Stearns who helped me set up my first website, *MujeresLatinas.com*, back in 1997, I will never be able to thank you enough. Many thanks to Michelle Generous, my first editor on *The Young Woman's Empowerment Journal*, and to Vincent Vanderbent, who designed the journal and served as both advisor and editor. Thanks also to Christie Ann Cappola for your thoughtful graphic designs.

Thank you to these respected authors whose books have inspired me to write and share my story: Sonia Sotomayor, Isabel Allende, Maria Hinojosa, Maria E. Martin, Sandra Cisneros, Julia Alvarez, Laura Esquivel, Sonia Sanchez, and Daisy Zamora, as I discover more to read.

The singers who inspired me in my youth are many. They begin with Sarah Vaughan, who I spent many nights singing along with her recordings as well as Anita O'Day, along with the many jazz singers. The Latin singers Graciela and Toña La Negra, the Brazilians Elis Regina and Flora

Purim how I spent many nights listening, learning and loving them for the motivation they inspired in me.

To the artist Geogia O'Keefe who left a lasting impression on me as a teenager, sparking a desire in me to live my life as an artist, which I'm still pursuing.

Thank you to the Latin jazz, jazz, and Brazilian musicians starting with Julie Janeiro who put the microphone in my hand and gave me my first live gig. And to my musical family of some who are now long gone—Aloisio Aguiar, Sergio Brandão, Guillerme Franco, Hélcio Milito for sharing musical love. To Nilson Mata, Romero Lubambo, Café, Portinho, and the extended family of the Brazilian music community of NYC. It's a chapter for Part 2 of my adventures.

To the incredible women who have been members of the *Mujeres Latinas* band: Rosy Rex, Flor Urrutia, Michelle Nestor, Orange Coffee (Katy Rodrigues), Johanna Castaneda, Kim Clark, Nicki Denner, Xiomara Gonzalez, Yasuyo Kimura, Heather Bennett, Anna Milat-Meyer, Pam Fleming, Jennifer Martinez, Deborah Resto, Bethina Flores, Santi Shan, Cecilia Tenconi, Annette Aguilar, and Jaie Timbalera—thank you.

To Frank Forti—for your photography, your MacGyverisms that always worked, and your help as my driver—thank you. And to James Amoroso—thank you for the little red Toyota that got me where I needed to go.

Special thanks to the great women who supported the *MujeresLatinas. com* project, helping to develop the empowerment workshop: Lourdes Torres and Millie Garcia. Also, to Maria Eugenia Speroni, Tanari Ponce, Patricia Matuk, and Lorena Garcia—thank you. To Nancy Rodrigues—thank you for always supporting women in music through your radio program on WBAI, New York.

A heartfelt thank you to Professor Janio Abreau Morcate for bringing me out of a long hiatus to sing again with the excellent students from the National School of Arts of Cuba. And to Emir Santa Cruz and Alejandro Falcón, for your assistance in that beautiful series of concerts in Cuba—thank you.

To Jorge Dalto, my first husband who brought me to New York City to begin my adventure of life. Juan Carlos Dalto and family, including my family in Roque Perez who will always be a part of my life.

Thank you to my sons, Billy and Miles, for being my pride and joy! To my siblings, including Louis Lezama; my granddaughters, Sofia and Adrianna; and my grandsons, Miles Jr., Dario, and Sebastian—you are all the heart of my inspiration for writing about my life's journey.

My Life Journey in Pictures

Here I am with my parents, sitting between my siblings, Sylvia and Joe (1954).

Here's one of the very few pictures as a child of four. I'm sitting between my sister Sylvia and my grandmother (1957). This picture survived a flood.

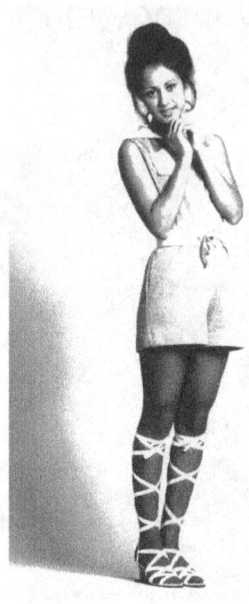

By the time I was 16 years old, I was told I could be a model, but I was also told I was too short and too Latina. What do you think? Here are some test shots.

The Fred Astaire dance competition in New York City in 1971, at seventeen.

I met Jorge in October 1972, and by February the following year we were married at City Hall in Chicago. We celebrated in the private poker room of the nightclub where he performed, sharing Roditi wine and lamb with his bandmates as our guests provided by the club manager. Later, it was showtime—Jorge and the band performed, while I danced the night away with friends.

Performing in my leather boots and showing off my baby bump (Argentina 1979).

Here we are on stage performing with bass player, Sal Cuevas (1984).

We Joined Jorge during one of his photo sessions (1982).

After Jorge passed, I had to take my own career seriously
because now I had to support the family.

Aloisio Aguiar Trio with Nilson Matta on Bass. (1990)

Brazilian Carnival Performance with Julie Janeiro, Anina, and fans.

On tour in Italy with Mario Bauza and the Afro Cuban Jazz Orchestra.

In Egypt on my famous but very short camel ride, 2004.

In Havana, Cuba, 2019.

In Cartagena, Colombia, 2025.

My granddaughters, Adrianna, and our sushi chef, Sofia, with their mother, Chelsy (2022).

On the Oregon coast with Miles jr., Sebi and daughter-in-law Jenny.

Sylvia, Mom and Dad, myself and Celia (2006).

My adorable grandsons Dario and Sebi (2021).

My sons Miles and Billy.

At 60 years old, the stars aligned for Bob and me to fall in love (2014).

Jamming in Harlem with Santi Debriano on bass, 2022.

Rehearsing students from the Nat'l School of the Arts, Cuba, 2023.

Performing with Rolando Briceño's Orchestra in NYC, 2024.

And the show continues...

About the Author

Adela Dalto Moraux, M.A., MHC, is a mental health counselor, vocalist, and world traveler who has visited over forty countries. She is the author of *The Young Woman's Empowerment Journal*, a workbook designed for high school students. To address the lack of role models and the high rates of suicidal ideation among young women, she created the website www.MujeresLatinas.com in 1997 to amplify the voices of notable Latinas as mentors and role models. She continues to advocate for women's empowerment.

With a bachelor's degree in music performance, Adela has released four Latin Jazz CDs: *A Brazilian Affair*, *Papa Boco* (released in Japan as *Peace*), *Exotica*, and *La Crème Latina*. She is featured in *Latin Jazz: The First of the Fusions, 1880s to Today* and *The Jazz Singers: The Ultimate Guide*. Her performances include New York's Rainbow Room, Jazz at Lincoln Center, the Blue Note, and Birdland. She has also appeared at major festivals, including the Puerto Rico Heineken Jazz Festival and the Clearwater Jazz

Festival, as well as events across Europe, Latin America, Japan, Indonesia, Egypt, and the Caribbean.

After a decade-long hiatus from singing to earn her master's degree and work as a mental health therapist, she returned to performing. She often says, "It's never too late to pick up where you left off."

Adela is an experienced speaker and workshop facilitator, introducing music and singing as therapeutic tools. She believes creativity is within everyone's reach.

She received a Lifetime Achievement Award from Governor George Pataki of New York in 2010. She enjoys her flower garden, languages, music, and reading—and cherishes time with her grandchildren. After thirty-five years of living in New York City, she remarried and now lives in Bucks County, Pennsylvania.

Keep the Journey Going with
Adela Dalto Moraux

Thank you for reading
Embracing Life, One Stage at a Time.

Your journey with me doesn't have to end here. There's still so much more to explore, share, and celebrate — together. Send your thoughts, reflections or notes directly to me at: **Adela@AuthorAdela.com**

Visit AuthorAdela.com for exclusive extras made just for readers like you.

Subscribe to the Newsletter and receive your free welcome gift:
The Reflection & Journaling Guide—created for you to thank you once again.

The website offers:

- Behind-the-scenes photos, songs & scrapbook pages

- Access to Adela's poems, videos, and more

- Printable quote cards & affirmations

- Empowerment tips for women of all ages

- Mental & physical wellness checklists

Visit music sites for **Adela Dalto,** the singer, before I became an author.

Take a tour at:

AuthorAdela.com	Tiktok: @mlmundo1
Mujereslatinas.com	Twitter: @mlmundo1
Instagram: @mlmundo1	Pandora: Adela Dalto
Facebook: @mlmundo1	Spotify: Adela Dalto

Invite the Author:

Adela Dalto Moraux is available for live and virtual events offering:

- Musical performances infused with storytelling

- Readings and reflections from my book

- Speaking engagements focused on culture, creativity, healing and wisdom in a presentation that uplifts and empowers your audience.

Write to the Author: Adela@AuthorAdela.com

- Ask Adela a question

- Book a 1-on-1 empowerment or life consultation

- Or to share your thoughts about my memoir

Contact: info@mlmundo.com

- To book Adela for an event

- Books in bulk

- Inquire about publishing support

Life moves forward. So do you.
With strength and light, step boldly.